To Brad Hatry, friend and enthusiast.

Merchant Ships of a Bygone Era
The Post-War Years

by

William H. Miller

Published by
Carmania Press
Unit 212, Station House, 49 Greenwich High Road, London SE10 8JL, Great Britain.

© William H. Miller and Carmania Press
ISBN 0 9518656 7 6
British Library Cataloguing for Publication Data.
A Catalogue Record for this book is available from the British Library.

Artwork production by Alan Kittridge.
First published 1997
Reprinted January 2001

Printed by The Amadeus Press, Cleckheaton.

Contents

Acknowledgements

A book of this diversity in ships and shipping activities could only have been compiled with the continued help and generous support of many friends, other individuals and organizations. I have merely been the catalyst, the organizer. Of course, I am immensely grateful to each of them. To all of you, over all the years and through many books of varied titles, a loud round of applause!

I am always grateful to Anthony Cooke and his Carmania Press for taking on these projects. They must be done. The photos must see the light of day. They are not only for us but also for the future enthusiasts, maritime historians, those spirited ship buffs of tomorrow. Since the steamship lines themselves have so often abandoned or simply discarded their photographic heritages, I am especially grateful to the great collectors. Among these, Frank Braynard is one of the World's greatest. Along with his own knowledge, he has so generously allowed me to pick through his enormous files of photographs, especially the cabinets marked 'Freighters and Other Non-Passenger Vessels'. Herein was a complete treasure chest of meticulous views, most of them grouped by vessel and by owner. I went off with folders of pictures, each one more fascinating and exciting than the next. I also had great assistance from Frank Duffy, formerly at Moran Towing & Transportation Company, and from Hisashi Noma, unquestionably Japan's foremost maritime author and historian.

Other photographers and photograph collectors who assisted include: Ernest Arroyo, Philippe Brebant, Michael Cassar, Luìs Miguel Correia, the late Frank Cronican, Alex Duncan, Laurence Dunn, Richard C. Faber, the late Alvin E. Grant, F. Leonard Jackson, Eric Johnson, Alan Kittridge, Peter Lancaric, Vincent Messina, C.B. Mulholland, Peter Newall, William Rau, Stanley Rawlings, Fred Rodriguez, Schiffsfotos Jansen, James L. Shaw, Roger Sherlock, Everett Viez, Steffen Weirauch, Joseph Wilhelm and V. H. Young. Companies and other organizations which assisted include the Alcoa Steamship Company, Compagnie Maritime Belge, Costa Line, Cunard-Ellerman Group, Ellerman Group, Flying Camera Inc, French Line, Matson Lines, Moran Towing & Transportation Company, P&O Group, the Port Authority of New York & New Jersey, the United States Department of Commerce and the World Ship Society. Other assistance came from the Erie Railroad, Holland-Africa Line, Royal Interocean Lines, Royal Mail Lines, Royal Netherlands Steamship Company, Royal Rotterdam Lloyd, Swedish Lloyd, Transports Maritimes, Union-Castle Line and the United Fruit Company – all, alas, no more.

Prized anecdotes and recollections came from a large source, among them: John Aldridge, Hans and Jule Andresen, Leslie Barton, Bill Burgers, Omer Cioli, Lewis and Ruth Gordon, Peter Houtmann, Captain Philip Jackson, Tom Johnson, Dr David Kirkman, Alastair Lloyd, Captain Hans Mateboer, Dean Miller, Eric Newman, Mike Northen, Robert Pelletier, Anthony Schiavone, Captain Heinz-Dieter Schmitt, Jan Solheim, Albert Stokes, Captain Ian Taylor and Captain Bill Wilson.

And last, but by no means least, my warmest thanks go to all my family and to my business partner, Abe Michaelson.

FRONT COVER: **The old gives way to the new. In this painting by Laurence Dunn, specially commissioned for this book, the year is 1947. We see one of the motor ships of the Blue Funnel Line's new *Anchises* class and, in the background, the Glen Line's veteran steamer *Gleniffer*, about to be withdrawn.**
BACK COVER: **American Export Lines advertisement 1950** *Alan Kittridge Collection.*
FRONTICE: **One of the best known and most popular passenger liners of all time, the majestic *Queen Mary* makes a midday departure from New York's 'Luxury Liner Row'. In this 1957 view, the 81,237-tonner is headed for Cherbourg and Southampton. On one of her regular 5-day Atlantic crossings, she carried over 1,900 passengers as well as some high-grade cargo. Apart from her status as one of the world's greatest ocean liners, the last of the 'three stackers' was also a ship of commerce.** *Frank Cronican Collection.*

Foreword

This is a book of pure nostalgia. It has been created as a pictorial parade of yesterday's shipping – the liners, the passenger-cargo combinations, the freighters and tankers, and even some early specialist types. It all covers the two or so decades after the Second World War, when worldwide shipping was revived and rebuilt, re-emerging bigger and better than ever. Along with a vast supply of wartime-built tonnage which was now wearing commercial colors, brand new ships came out of shipyards at an unparalleled pace. If freighters grew somewhat, oil tankers rocketed to what would have been unimaginable proportions – bigger and bigger still! European shipyards, in particular British yards, were dominant in the late 1940s and '50s. The great shipowners were back in business again: Cunard, the French Line, the Italian Line, United States Lines, Moore-McCormack, Grace, Royal Mail, Union-Castle, Farrell, P&O, British India, NYK – to name but a starting dozen.

But tremendous changes were said to be ahead and all of them began in 1957. Two changes would affect the shipping business like nothing perhaps since the technological transition from sail to steam. In the business of running passenger ships, the airlines equalled for the first time the number of travellers who went by sea on the North Atlantic routes. It was the beginning of the end for those long-established trades between such ports as New York, Montreal and Halifax, and Southampton, Liverpool, Le Havre, Rotterdam, Lisbon and Naples. Then, in the Fall of '58, PanAm started the first commercial jet service across the Atlantic and the fate of passenger ships everywhere was sealed. Within six months on the Atlantic, the airlines had two-thirds of the clientele; by 1965, they had as much as 95%. The Cunard Queens, as major examples, sailed off into retirement in 1967 and '68. The airlines later dominated all other sea routes as well: trans-Pacific, South Atlantic and all those going east of Suez. Decolonization, spiralling operational costs and the shift of precious and very lucrative cargo from combination passenger-cargo liners to faster, more efficient containerships (some of them flying Third World colors) also contributed to what, looking back, seems to have been a quick demise. One of the last holdouts, Union-Castle Line's South African passenger and mail service, finally closed down in 1977. Thereafter, the passenger ship business primarily became the cruise ship business.

Secondly, in 1957, the converted *Gateway City* entered service. With a capacity of 226 35-foot containers, she was considered the World's first full containership. Proving efficient, she was placed, however, in short-sea service between US and Caribbean ports. But her practicality and profitability soon influenced others to build larger and larger ships. Nine years later was dubbed 'Year 1' of the international maritime transport of containers. Everyone was making the changeover – even great traditionalists like Cunard and P&O. A year later, in 1967, the first full containership crossed the Atlantic. Almost immediately, 'second generation' ships were ordered, for 1,000 and then 1,500 containers each. By 1969, the giant, powerful *Sea-Land Galloway* class were being built – 33-knot, high-capacity containerships. That same year, the first barge-carrying ship, the *Acadia Forest*, went into service. Two years later, in 1971, the *Paralla* was commissioned. She was the first pure, deep-sea freight ro-ro (roll-on, roll-off) ship. Technologically, the revolution had come. Today, containerships, ro-ros and specialty freighters ply routes across the globe. And as the world population increases so does the need for maritime transport. As this book was in progress, the Japanese, namely the NYK and Mitsui-OSK lines, were taking delivery of the largest containerships to date, six ships with capacities of 4,800 'boxes' each. But Denmark's Maersk Line have since built a series of 6,000-capacity containerships. Old-style breakbulk freighters are rare sights these days.

1957 was also the year of the World's first nuclear-powered merchant ship, the *Savannah* She was laid down at a shipyard near Philadelphia. Launched in 1960 and then completed two years later, the 14,000-ton, 60-passenger combination ship was said to be the beginning of whole nuclear fleets. Germany, Japan and others were making plans for ships of their own. Even the brand new *Leonardo Da Vinci*, a 33,000-ton luxury liner completed in the Spring of 1960, was said to be convertible from steam turbine to nuclear propulsion. Confident, her Italian owners predicted that the changeover would probably take place within five years. But nuclear power in the commercial shipping sector proved troublesome, costly, inefficient. Never pleasing to the accountants, the *Savannah* was decommissioned within eight years, by 1970, and later turned into a museum ship. More recently, in 1994, she joined the Government's 'mothball fleet' in Virginia's James River, a sad reminder of her great promise in the late 1950s.

But back to those golden days of the 1950s and my own weakness (and I think others' as well) for things past and some gone forever. I have divided this photographic collection into nine sections. The first five are themed geographically to ships and shipowners and some of the ports they served. The next two chapters, 6 and 7, deal with the transport of oil and special cargos. The final two sections examine the life cycle of the ship – shipbuilding, ship repair and ship breaking.

These days, when I look out over New York harbor or visit such ports as London-Tilbury, Southampton, Le Havre, Lisbon, Genoa, Sydney and Yokohama, it is easy to see the great changes. Harbor waters are much quieter, sometimes quite empty. Many of the old docks and dockyards are gone, some replaced by marinas, waterside shops and fancy housing. Containerships come and go far less often and then to more distant facilities with vast spaces and served by those big, bird-like cranes. But sometimes, I dream. I can still see the *Queen Mary* or the *Ile De France*, an American Export freighter, a United Fruit banana boat in drydock. I hope this book will be a small reminder of a fabulous era.

Bill Miller,
Secaucus, New Jersey, Fall 1996

Chapter One
Trans-Atlantic

When getting there was half the fun: The Cunard Line

When John Aldridge emigrated from his native England to a 'new life' in America in 1954, he landed at New York in what was then the biggest ocean liner afloat, Cunard Line's original *Queen Elizabeth*. She was well over 83,000 tons, 1,031 feet in length and could carry 2,233 passengers. The airlines had yet to overtake the steamship companies and so lines like Cunard were thriving. With a dozen passenger ships of their own and therefore with the biggest chunk of North Atlantic traffic, they enthusiastically boasted that on their class-divided ships (first, cabin and tourist on the old 'Elizabeth' and her running-mate, the *Queen Mary*) 'getting there was half the fun.' Indeed it was. Hearty English breakfasts, shuffleboard, ritualized teas, a good book in one of those old wooden deckchairs and all the while tucked-in by a cheerfully attendant steward with a great tartan blanket that the English (and Cunard) called a 'rug'. For Americans, it was the exciting beginning of a European visit and then, on return, the rest after a busy tour. Then, of course, there were the Hollywood stars, the frontpage politicians, the corporate chiefs, even royalty who used the Cunarders, as they were called, for pure but very pampered transport.

"The two big Queens were marvellous ships – absolutely floating cities. 2,000 passengers and 1,000 crew on those 5-day express runs between New York and Southampton and with a quick stop at Cherbourg each way. You'd leave New York on Wednesday and then be in London by Monday evening. But one particular crossing stands out in my memory," noted Mr. Aldridge. "It was

October 1954 and I was returning to England on the *Queen Mary*. Among the passengers was the Queen Mother, that grand lady who is now well into her nineties. She was returning from an official visit to Canada and the States. Royalty still didn't travel by air very often. She had gone over weeks before on the 'Elizabeth'. Onboard the 'Mary', she was always a very gracious lady, talking to everyone, visiting all parts of the ship. She often attended children's tea parties. She was constantly seen, always out and available. She travelled about with a small entourage. And she always wore her trademark flowery hats."

Two occasions remain in John Aldridge's memory from that special royal crossing. "The Queen Mother attended the ship's Sunday church service. It was so crowded they couldn't admit all the passengers. The Queen Mother stood during the entire service and so no one else dared to sit. During the trip, the *Queen Elizabeth* was especially routed on her way to New York so that she would pass within a quarter-of-a-mile of the *Queen Mary*. It was daylight and both ships were dressed overall in flags. Both ships were doing some 30 knots and so it was a combined 60 knot encounter. Two monsters were passing. The whistles were deafening. There was cheering. Cameras were going like mad. The Queen Mother was on the bridge. It was a great day for Britain and a great day for Cunard!"

After the 5-day passage, tugs nudged the three-stack *Queen Mary* into Southampton's Ocean Terminal. The Queen Mother and her party were among the first to go ashore. John Aldridge soon followed, up to London on the famed, but long gone 'boat train' to Waterloo Station. "In honor of the Queen Mother's arrival, Customs didn't check. Everyone just passed through. It was a great time for smugglers!"

They were the greatest pair of liners ever to sail the North Atlantic. In this 1949 view (opposite top) **the *Queen Mary* is being docked by no less than seven Moran tugboats. She is arriving at Cunard's New York terminal, Pier 90, at West 50th Street. Just behind her stern is the French Line's *De Grasse*. Her slightly larger running-mate, the *Queen Elizabeth*, is shown outbound in 1957** (opposite bottom). **At 83,673 tons, she was the largest passenger ship ever built. Completed in 1940, she was not surpassed until the arrival of the first 100,000-ton cruiseships in 1996-97.** *Both photographs: Port Authority of New York & New Jersey.*

Sailings from New York, June 1951

Friday, June 1st
Homeland, Home Lines; Southampton, Hamburg . . . . . 11:30am . . . . 97 HR W 57 st
Santa Rosa, Grace Line; Caribbean. . . . . Noon . . . . 58 HR W 16 st
Santa Clara, Grace Line; Caribbean . . . . 11:30am . . . . 45 HR W 10 st
Santa Margarita, Grace Line; South America . . . . Noon . . . . 58 HR W 16 st
Antigua, United Fruit; Central America. . . . . 3:00pm . . . . Morris st

Saturday, June 2nd
Noordam, Holland America; Rotterdam . . . . Noon . . . . 5th st, Hoboken
Ocean Monarch, Furness; Bermuda . . . . 3:00pm . . . . 95 HR W 55 st
Brazil, Moore-McCormack; South America . . . . Noon . . . . 23 HR Canal st

Sunday, June 3rd
No sailings

Monday, June 4th
No sailings

Tuesday, June 5th
Batory, Gdynia America; Gdynia . . . . Noon . . . . 88 HR W 48 st

Wednesday, June 6th
Ancon, Panama Line; Cristobal. . . . . 3:00pm . . . . 64 HR W 24 st
Rio De La Plata, Argentine State; Buenos Aires . . . . 5:00pm . . . . 25 HR Franklin st
Atlantic, Home Lines; Genoa, Naples. . . . . 11:30am . . . . 54 HR W 14 st

Thursday, June 7th
Mauretania, Cunard; Southampton . . . . 3:30pm . . . . 90 HR W 50 st
Queen Elizabeth, Cunard; Southampton. . . . . 9:00pm . . . . 90 HR W 50 st
Puerto Rico, Bull Insular; Caribbean . . . . 3:00pm . . . . 21st St, Brooklyn

Friday, June 8th
Veendam, Holland America; Rotterdam. . . . . Noon . . . . 5th st, Hoboken
Gripsholm, Swedish American; Gothenburg. . . . . 10:30am . . . . 97 HR W 57 st
Exeter, American Export; Mediterranean . . . . 4:00pm . . . . F, Jersey City
Vulcania, Italian; Mediterranean. . . . . Noon . . . . 84 HR W 44 st
Nieuw Amsterdam, Holland America; Rotterdam . . . . . . 4:00pm . . . . 5th st, Hoboken
Media, Cunard; Liverpool. . . . . 3:30pm . . . . 54 HR W 14 st
Talamanca, United Fruit; Central America . . . . 3:00pm . . . . Morris st
Santa Paula, Grace; Caribbean. . . . . Noon . . . . 58 HR W 16 st
Santa Sofia, Grace; Caribbean . . . . 11:30am . . . . 45 HR W 10 st
Santa Barbara, Grace; Caribbean . . . . Noon . . . . 58 HR W 16 st

Saturday, June 9th
Ile De France, French Line; Le Havre . . . . Noon . . . . 88 HR W 48 st
Ocean Monarch, Furness; Bermuda . . . . 3:00pm . . . . 95 HR W 55 st

Sunday, June 10th
No sailings

Monday, June 11th
Nea Hellas, Greek Line; Piraeus . . . . Noon . . . . 4th st, Hoboken

The French Line to Europe

"You always met the chic-est people and saw the most fabulously dressed women in first class on the old French Line to and from Europe," recalled Lewis and Ruth Gordon, who crossed on the *Ile De France*, the *Liberté* and the *France*. "These ships also had some of the greatest and grandest public rooms – two- and three-deck high lounges, Aubusson carpets and impressive stairways."

"And the kitchens were justifiably famous. Passengers actually used to vie with one another to produce special recipes that could stump the chefs. They never did, of course, but sometimes these items might appear on the regular menu two days later. I especially remember Chicken Subarov," noted Mr. Gordon. "A whole chicken was baked in clay. The juices were contained within and then they'd break the clay and serve the chicken. And the caviar flowed freely. They used those one pound boxes of Beluga and served it with a soup spoon. There were three bottles of wine at every table – red, white and rosé. They came from the French Line's own vineyards. And when you had the fish course, the waiter would skin and bone it at his serving counter. And, of course, you could have Filet Mignon for breakfast if you wanted. Our sons, who ate

The splendid *Ile De France*, a three-funnel liner when first built in 1927 and then remodelled after the Second World War, prepares to dock at New York's Pier 88. She was one of the most celebrated liners on the North Atlantic run in the 1950s. One of her fleetmates, the smaller *Flandre*, and American Export Lines' *Independence* are docked in the background. *Frank O. Braynard Collection.*

The North German Lloyd record-breaker *Europa*, built in 1930, was ceded to the French as reparations in 1946 and became their *Liberté*. After extensive refitting, she resumed trans-Atlantic sailings in the summer of 1950. Like the *Ile De France*, she was especially known for her onboard luxury, her fine service and her flawless kitchens. *Fred Rodriguez Collection.*

separately from us later confessed that they ate three Filet Mignons a day – at breakfast, at lunch and at dinner. Another passenger called room service at 1 in the morning on the *France*, ordered a lobster and it was delivered. It was no joke when they said that the French Line ships dumped the best leftovers over the sides!"

The 44,000-ton *Ile De France*, a celebrated pre-War liner, was revived and restored in 1949 after strenuous military trooping. The 51,000-ton *Liberté*, which had been Germany's record-breaking *Europa* in the '30s, came to the French as reparations and, after heavy shipyard surgery, first appeared in 1950. They each carried the then traditional three classes: first, cabin and tourist. Peak summer season one-way fares in 1960 started at $400 in first class. The *Ile De France* and the *Liberté* sailed almost all the year between New York, Southampton or Plymouth and Le Havre. A third ship, the 20,000-ton *Flandre*, helped out beginning in 1953, but she was considered to be primarily a tourist class ship.

The 'Ile' went to Japanese scrappers in 1959 and the *Liberté* to Italian wreckers three years later. They were replaced by the stunningly new, 66,000-ton *France*, which carried approximately 500 in first class and 1,500 in tourist. "She was, of course, a modern ship," noted Mr. Gordon, "and so she was not quite as grand as either the 'Ile' or the *Liberté*. The *Liberté* was, in fact, always our favorite for the French Line. The new *France* had a shorter grand staircase, for example, into her first class restaurant. The room itself was magnificent and was called the Chambord. Of course, the *France* always had fabulous food – the very best afloat in those days! We were sad to see her go."

The 1,035-foot long *France* was laid-up in September 1974, when French Line decided to end all trans-Atlantic and cruise services. Airline competition, economics and the loss of a much-needed subsidy from Paris were the reasons. For five years, she sat in a Le Havre backwater before Norwegian Caribbean Lines bought her and transformed her into the *Norway* for Caribbean cruising.

Quartermaster of the 'Big U'

"Sometimes, in a 'following sea' or 'following wind', she would lift at the stern and her props would not grab as much. At other times, and usually with other quartermasters, she would 'get away from them'. She would even swing off course. Then, once you tried to rectify this, she'd begin to 'yaw.' The superliner *United States* was a very sensitive ship, but she responded very quickly." These are just some recollections from Leslie Barton, the chief quartermaster of the World's fastest ocean liner, the brilliant *SS United States*. He was with her during her entire American sailing career – from the record-breaking, 3½-day maiden voyage in July 1952 to her very last crossing in November 1969. Laid-up at Norfolk, Virginia for nearly 23 years, she was finally auctioned off to Turkish buyers and so was towed to a small port near Istanbul in the summer of 1992. In 1996 she was taken back to the USA. She now waits – perhaps to undergo a costly resurrection as a cruiseship. But the 990-foot long ship remains of great interest to many.

Barton had had considerable experience with big ocean liners. "I started on the old *Leviathan*, one of the biggest ships afloat, back in 1934. I began as a dishwasher. I earned $28 a month and brought my own fork, knife and plate, and a straw mattress bed." He later joined other passenger ships of some of the great names of American shipping: the Panama Pacific Line, the Grace Line, Moore-McCormack and of course the United

Outbound on her triumphant, record-breaking eastbound maiden voyage on July 3rd 1952, the brilliant *United States* heads for the Lower Bay, the open Atlantic and finally Southampton. She is seen passing the inbound cruiseship *Nassau*, the former P&O liner *Mongolia*. Primarily because of her cachet as the 'World's fastest passenger ship', the 990-foot long *United States* was the most popular single liner on the Atlantic run in the '50s. *Moran Towing & Transportation Company.*

States Lines. During the Second World War, he served on the converted Moore-McCormack cruiseship *Uruguay*. "We carried over 5,000 troops all the way from New York to Melbourne, Australia. We zigzagged all the way, endured food shortages and even ran out of fresh water."

After the War, Barton stayed with the *Uruguay* for a time, in war bride service and later on the luxury run to South America. He later joined the United States Lines and was assigned to the spectacular *United States* just in time for her maiden voyage. He was also there for the unannounced last voyage. "After her very last trip, from New York down to the Newport News Shipyard, I was the last person to ring-up 'Finished With Engines'. She never sailed again. But I didn't fully realize it was the very last time."

In earlier days, there were some difficult moments for the 1,725-passenger pride of the US merchant fleet. According to Les Barton, "Normal docking took no more than 45 minutes. But during tugboat strikes, when we docked ourselves, it took 2½ hours. I remember a huge North Atlantic hurricane when we lost the searchlights on the foward kingposts, several bridge windows were cracked and great waves poured over the bow. And sometimes going along the Weser River in Germany could be very risky. It was very shallow and we were always worried about touching bottom. Once at Kingston, Jamaica, during a cruise, we bent a propeller blade. On another occasion, during our big South Atlantic cruise, we were at Port Elizabeth in South Africa. There was rather poor tug service there and a 'Southerner' came up from the Antarctic region. 'Big U' was broadside to the wind and just held against the dock. Those two big stacks were just like sails. We couldn't get away. We sailed late that evening and so had to make up time. As we rounded the Cape of Good Hope, a South African Air Force fighter plane called down. He couldn't believe we were doing 40 knots. We needed to get to Luanda in Angola on schedule. Someone else recalled 41 knots, but I can't verify this. What fun it was to sail in the fastest liner afloat!"

American Export to the Mediterranean & Beyond

It was often said that once every 24 hours one of the 29 ships flying the colors of the American Export Lines passed Gibraltar. These ships were bound from the East Coast of the United States to just about every port in the Mediterranean and even some beyond Suez. In all, the New York-headquartered company had eight different routes so as to cover the entire length and width of the Mediterranean. These included the express passenger service to Spain, Italy and the south of France (run by the 29,500-ton liners *Independence* and *Constitution*) and cargo services into the Adriatic, the Black Sea, along the North African coast and the eight ships that sailed to India, Ceylon and East Pakistan. American Export's Hoboken Terminal was often filled with ships and their cargoes.

This view, from the early 1960s and after American Export had been merged as the American Export-Isbrandtsen Lines, shows three ships at Hoboken. The hold in the foreground belongs to a new vessel, the very efficient *Export Ambassador*; beyond is the Wartime-built *Exbrook*; and farther still, the stack and masts of the combination passenger-cargo ship *Exeter*. Loading and unloading continued throughout the day and often well into the night. *Flying Camera Inc.*

(opposite) **During the Second World War, American Export started a large building program of new cargo liners. The first of these, a quartet, were built in 1941-42 by the Bath Iron Works in Maine. They were named the *Exceller*, *Extavia* (shown passing the lower Manhattan skyline and bound for a six-week voyage to the Mediterranean), *Exanthia* and *Exiria*. At 6,500 tons, they measured 420 feet in length, had speeds of 16$\frac{1}{2}$ knots and were quite novel for their use of the classic counter stern in otherwise contemporary freighters. The *Extavia* was actually completed just in time to go on Lend Lease to the British and sailed for about a year as the *Empire Oriole*. She reverted to American operation and her original name afterwards, and then was converted to a US Government transport with a capacity for as many as 1,360 troops. She entered American Export commercial service in the winter of 1946 and sailed for them until broken-up in Spain in 1968.** *Frank O. Braynard Collection.*

Changing Names

The American Export Lines were not 'big contenders' in the transatlantic passenger business, at least in their early years. Mostly, they seemed to be content with a fleet of two dozen or so freighters, some of which carried 12 passengers, and a quartet of slightly larger ships, known as the 'Four Aces.' Named *Excalibur*, *Excambion*, *Exeter* and *Exochorda*, these ships carried about 125 passengers each, all in rather high standard first class quarters. All of these Export ships plied the mid-Atlantic route to Mediterranean ports and sometimes beyond Suez to India. But in the late 'forties, in that age of high Yankee prosperity and expansion following the Second World War, the Company took a rather bold step: they ordered two 29,000-ton liners. Each would carry 1,000 passengers, divided in the then traditional pattern of three classes: first, cabin and tourist.

Built by the well-known Bethlehem Steel Company at their Quincy, Massachusetts plant, the *Independence* was the first and slid down the ways in June 1950. To the cheers of thousands and with Washington as a financial benefactor, she launched a new era for American ocean liners. A sister, the *Constitution*, would soon follow and then there would be United States Lines' extraordinary *United States*, the fastest liner ever built. Triumphantly carrying the Stars and Stripes, each of these ships would enjoy about a decade of high profit.

The *Independence* shuttled back and forth out of New York, mostly on three-week round voyages to Algeciras, Naples, Genoa and Cannes. Sample tourist class fares for the 1962 summer season began at $289, and at $334 for cabin and $421 in first. A 44-day mid-winter Mediterranean cruise had a minimum of $1245.

In the 'sixties, as American labor costs soared and as passengers began to defect to the airlines, the *Independence* began to fall on hard times. There were more cruises and a remake of the ship (with an overwhelming psychedelic repainting) in 1968. Called the 'art disco era', there were 7-day Caribbean cruises for $98 but sans food! A year later, the 683-foot liner was laid-up at Baltimore – out of work and looking for a new owner.

Finally bought by the C.Y. Tung Group of Hong Kong and Taiwan in 1974, she was rechristened *Oceanic Independence*, but for a long time did little apart from evacuating some Portugese nationals out of newly independent Angola. Laid-up near Hong Kong, she was later refurbished and reactivated in 1980, and then joined Tung's American Hawaii Cruises for weekly island cruises out of Honolulu. Three years later, having been joined by the *Constitution*, the *Oceanic Independence* reverted to her original name. Again proud and profitable, and the subject of a new commemorative book, the *Independence* continues to carry her great name.

(above) **The American Export cargo ship *Exchester* has just returned to home waters after a ten-week round voyage out to India, Ceylon and East Pakistan. From Bombay, she has returned with cotton waste, gum, crude talc, goatskins, cashew nuts and bones; from Colombo, there are tea, rubber and cinnamon; and from Karachi, there are wool, pistachio nuts and celery seeds. But once unloaded, she will be off on a 10-day 'coastal swing', touching at Philadelphia, Baltimore and Hampton Roads before returning to New York to load her final outbound cargo for another long journey out East. American Export was among the last major shipping lines to use the traditional counter stern.** *Frank O. Braynard Collection.*

(opposite) **In this April 1964 view, the *Constitution* arrives at New York's 'Luxury Liner Row' with the *United States*, the *Berlin*, the *Queen Elizabeth*, the *Homeric* and the *Empress of Canada* in the background.** *Frank O. Braynard Collection.*

Three American Export ships are seen in this aerial view dating from July 1961. The 125-passenger combo liner *Exeter* is to the left, in port between 42-day round voyages to the Mediterranean. The brand new, 12-passenger *Export Agent* is in the centre. She was then one of the first ships in the Company's rebuilding program. Along with a higher cargo capacity and greater speed, she had far more efficient cargo-handling equipment than her 1945-46 built fleetmates. On the far right is the *Exhibitor*, one of those post-War freighters which were then passing into obsolescence. *Port Authority of New York & New Jersey.*

The Norwegian-flag freighters of the Meyer Line ran a regular North Atlantic service from New York, Hampton Roads, Baltimore and Philadelphia to Antwerp, Rotterdam, Amsterdam, Bremen and Hamburg. With sailings every 10 days from New York and other U.S. ports, their breakbulk freighter services ran from the end of the Second World War until the early 1970s, when they were discontinued in face of containerization. Poetically, in a late afternoon scene and with some early containers secured both fore and aft, the *Havsul* heads out to sea on another voyage to Northern Europe. *Frank O. Braynard Collection.*

Among other trans-Atlantic freighter companies, the Swedish-flag Thorden Lines ran a regular service, sailing from New York every Friday to Copenhagen, Malmo and Gothenburg. They used such ships as the 5,500-ton *Clary Thorden* (pictured), the *Hjordis Thorden* and *Selma Thorden.*

The Danish-flag Torm Lines used such ships as the 6-passenger *Estrid Torm* in service to the Mediterranean and North Africa.
both photographs: Alex Duncan.

Apart from such well known passenger liners as the *United States* and the *America*, the United States Lines had over 50 freighters at their peak in the 1950s. These included numerous C-2 class ships such as the *American Harvester* which was built in 1944. With accommodations for 12 passengers along with five holds of freight, she measured 459 feet in length, 8,300 gross tons and could make a regular 16 knots. *Alex Duncan.*

In another view, the *American Chief* (right) is moored across from a near-sister, the *American Ranger*, at one of United States Lines' Hudson River piers. In the foreground is the *Catherine McAllister*. McAllisters were one of New York's most important tug fleets. *Frank O. Braynard Collection.*

Immediately after the Second World War demand for cargo space was exceeding high and shipowners ran many chartered ships. Here the C-1 class *Cape Trafalgar* is shown at New York, being readied to take on a large consignment of trucks, which are bound for Holland and Germany. *Frank O. Braynard Collection.*

United States Lines
Freighter Sailings April 1951

ship	from New York	to	ship	from New York	to
American Veteran	Mon Apr 2	Plymouth, Bremerhaven	*American Chief*	Mon Apr 16	Liverpool
American Press	Thu Apr 5	Plymouth, Bremerhaven	*American Miller*	Tue Apr 17	Bremerhaven
American Leader	Fri Apr 6	Bremerhaven	*American Reporter*	Fri Apr 20	Plymouth, Cherbourg, Bremerhaven
American Shipper	Sat Apr 7	Le Havre			
American Traveler	Mon Apr 9	Liverpool	*American Defender*	Fri Apr 20	Antwerp
American Judge	Mon Apr 9	Antwerp	*American Scout*	Sun Apr 22	Liverpool
American Farmer	Tue Apr 10	Bremerhaven	*American Merchant*	Tue Apr 24	Bremerhaven
American Importer	Thu Apr 12	Plymouth, Bremerhaven	*American Scientist*	Thu Apr 26	Plymouth, Bremerhaven
American Packer	Thu Apr 12	Liverpool	*American Harvester*	Fri Apr 27	Le Havre
American Banker	Fri Apr 13	Le Havre	*American Counselor*	Sat Apr 28	Antwerp
American Lawyer	Sat Apr 14	Antwerp	*American Forwarder*	Mon Apr 30	Liverpool

Not all Cunarders were passenger ships. The *Andria*, for example, was one of two all-cargo ships acquired from the Silver Line in 1952 for the North Atlantic trade between London, New York and other ports. The 1948-built, 7,200-ton *Andria* was the former *Silverbriar*; her sister *Alsatia* was originally the *Silverplane*. Together with the *Assyria*, *Asia* and the *Arabia*, they made up what was known as Cunard's 'A' fleet. The forward funnel on the *Andria* as well as on the *Alsatia* was a dummy; it contained part of the wheelhouse and the radio room. *Alex Duncan.*

A decade or so later, a new generation of freighters joined Cunard's North Atlantic services. These included the engines-aft *Media*, shown being assisted by Moran tugs as she arrives at New York's Pier 94, Cunard's cargo-only terminal at West 54th Street, on October 28th 1963. But her days were shortened. By the late 1960s, Cunard was planning to abandon its trans-Atlantic breakbulk freighter services and join a new consortium known as the Atlantic Container Line. *Frank O. Braynard Collection.*

A Pier in Brooklyn

These days, New York harbor is often quite lonely. Gone are the busy days of tall-stacked ferries, freight car-laden railway carfloats, cargo-filled barges and steam-sprouting floating derricks. They served a vast fleet that included the great trans-Atlantic liners, international freighters and, in the Port's outer waters, heavily-laden oil tankers. Today, there are only three active piers along Manhattan's western shore, in that vast stretch from Battery Park to West 57th Street, the end of 'Luxury Liner Row'. But some fifty years ago, as the Second World War ended in 1945, there were 102 very active piers all around Manhattan Island. There were dozens more in nearby Brooklyn, Jersey City, Hoboken, Weehawken and Staten Island. Most shipowners preferred the convenience and prestige of a New York City berth, but it was simply not possible for all. And so, while the likes of the Holland America Line used Hoboken and American President called at Jersey City, other lines looked to Brooklyn.

The Zim Lines was started in 1947, and became the official shipping company of the infant state of Israel. They began a rather erratic trans-Atlantic passenger service six years later, using an old liner, once Norwegian America Line's original *Bergensfjord* (built in 1913), which they re-named *Jerusalem*. But by 1955, a West German reparations pact provided new passenger tonnage, namely a quartet of ships – the 9,800-ton passenger-cargo sisters *Israel* and *Zion*, and then a pair of sisters with at least some off-season cruising in mind, the 9,900-ton *Jerusalem* and *Theodor Herzl*. For these ships, the Zim Lines used the Kent Street pier in the Greenpoint section of Brooklyn. A 600-foot long dock, it was located just across the East River from 23rd Street in Manhattan.

The 17-knot *Israel* and *Zion* called about every three weeks, sailing between Brooklyn, Madeira, Gibraltar, Naples, Piraeus and finally Haifa. Along with a considerable amount of freight, they carried 312 passengers at capacity – 24 in first class and the rest in tourist. In the late 1950s, the first class for the 14-day trip to Haifa was priced from $330; tourist berths started at $255. The 487-foot long *Jerusalem* called only in winter, especially for cruising to the sunny Caribbean. A sample voyage, 9 days to Cap Haitien, San Juan and St Thomas, was priced from $185 in 1959.

Zim was joined at the Kent Street pier in 1958 by the liner *Atlantic*, a 14,100-ton, 880-passenger ship that had just been converted from a freighter for the North Atlantic service of the shortlived American Banner Lines. Offering a high standard of nevertheless economical tourist class travel (which included private shower and toilet in even the least expensive cabins), she ran a year-round service to Zeebrugge (in Belgium) and Amsterdam. Within less than a year, however, American Banner subleased space at Piers 95-97, then the home of the Furness-Bermuda and Swedish American Lines. Later in 1959, the company closed and the *Atlantic* was sold to American Export Lines. Zim followed to the Manhattan waterfront in 1961, when they took over Pier 64, at West 24th Street, the former Panama Line terminal. (Later, in 1964, when the brand new, 25,000-ton *Shalom* arrived, they went south, to the longer Pier 32 at Canal Street. It had been previously used by the Moore-McCormack Lines.)

In the early '60s, the Kent Street pier in Brooklyn had one other passenger ship tenant, the Spanish Line. They ran two motorliners, the 10,200-ton *Covadonga* and *Guadalupe*. These two-class ships (with some 350 total berths) ran a unique triangular trans-Atlantic service between Spain, New York and the Caribbean and Mexico. But they soon relocated as well, moving to the Harborside Terminal in Jersey City.

After a few cargo firms came and went, the Kent Street pier was eventually closed and then gradually fell into disrepair and decay. A fire damaged part of it and then the centre section began to sag and sink. Today, it is a sad, lonely sight, but yet a reminder to some of us of far busier, happier, perhaps more romantic times in New York harbor.

Zim Lines' *Zion* is here seen in New York harbor.
Peter Newall Collection.

A banner day for the Greek-flag Hellenic Lines as five of their cargoships are berthed at 56th and 57th Streets in Brooklyn. The Company had weekly sailings to the Mediterranean and to the Middle East. Later a victim of financial over-extension, Hellenic Lines went bankrupt in the early 1980s. *Fred Rodriguez Collection.*

Because of the shortage of suitable ships in the years immediately following the Second World War, many older vessels were given extended lives. In this case, the 6,856-ton *Pulaski* of the Polish-flag Gdynia America Line is shown leaving the Todd Shipyard in Hoboken, New Jersey (just across from the New York City skyline). The date is March 25, 1948 and she has just completed an expensive, four-month conversion and refit. She has been changed from coal to oil burning, and her midship house has been modified to accommodate a dozen passengers for North Atlantic service. The 459-foot long ship was used thereafter as a direct link between Gdynia, Copenhagen and such North American ports as Halifax, Boston, New York, Baltimore and Philadelphia.
Frank O. Braynard Collection.

Swedish American Line's handsome *Stureholm*, an 8,800-tonner built in 1957, not only sailed the Company's North Atlantic freight and passenger routes, but served as a fleet training ship. Her accommodations included space for two dozen maritime cadets. *Alex Duncan.*

One of the first new passenger ships to be built after the Second World War was the 12,000-ton Swedish American passenger-cargo liner *Stockholm*. Although completed in 1948, she was actually ordered and designed before the War was over, in 1944, and then launched two years later. A smallish passenger ship by North Atlantic standards, she was noted at the time of her debut as the largest vessel yet built in Sweden and also for the special strengthening of her hull for winter passages between Gothenburg and New York. She went on to achieve something of maritime immortality when, on July 25th 1956, she collided with the Italian Line flagship *Andrea Doria* in heavy fog off the Massachusetts coast. After lengthy repairs, she later became the East German trade union cruiseship *Volkerfreundschaft* and sails to this day, but as the completely rebuilt Italian cruiseship *Italia Prima*. She is shown being docked as the *Stockholm* at New York's Pier 97 in 1951, with the Swedish freighter *Oklahoma* to the far right. *Moran Towing & Transportation Company.*

St Lawrence Sailing

On a cruise sailing one recent summer, the sleek, luxurious cruiseship *Seabourn Pride* entered Canada's mighty St Lawrence River just after midnight. So wide, we could see only the pin-dot lights of one side. The next morning, off our port bow, was the skyline of Quebec City. There were skyscrapers above the treetops. We cruised past Ile d'Orléans, several inbound freighters and then the shipyards at Lauzon. Finally, the stately Château Frontenac Hotel came into full view and then, in its shadows just below, our berth. Momentarily, our arrival brought back memories of earlier, perhaps busier times of shipping on the St Lawrence.

The last great heyday for the Atlantic liners serving Eastern Canada was the late 1950s and early '60s. Expectedly, British ships dominated the trade. Cunard alone had four liners serving Quebec City (as well as Montreal) in the ice-free season that extended from April until early December. The 22,000-ton, 900-passenger *Saxonia* and *Ivernia* (later renamed *Carmania* and *Franconia*) sailed out of London, Southampton, Le Havre and Cobh while their sisters, the *Carinthia* and *Sylvania*, maintained an alternative service out of Liverpool and Greenock (Scotland). Their trade consisted mostly of migrants westbound and then gradually fewer tourists in reverse.

Cunard's main rivals were the last Empress liners of Canadian Pacific – the sisters *Empress of Britain* and *Empress of England*, and then the flagship *Empress of Canada*. These ships traded out of Liverpool and Greenock.

The Holland America Line then also maintained a regular St Lawrence service, using their *Ryndam* from Rotterdam, Le Havre and Southampton, as did the now defunct Greek Line with their *Arkadia* (a ship not to be confused with P&O's bigger *Arcadia* of the same era). The *Arkadia* included the Channel ports along with Amsterdam and Bremerhaven. Then there were also the Poles with the pre-War *Batory*. But it all began to wind down as the jets took an increasingly firm hold. Cunard withdrew in 1967 and Canadian Pacific followed four years later. Another Polish liner, the *Stefan Batory*, ran the last regular Atlantic crossings out of Canada in 1987.

Early cruises to the St Lawrence region and in particular to Quebec City were rather limited. Ships like the *Gripsholm* and the *Ocean Monarch* made occasional summertime visits out of New York in the 1950s. In the '60s, giant liners such as the *France* and the *Michelangelo*, also made special calls, and then there have been several, even more recent appearances by the *QE2*. Presently, no less than a dozen cruiseships are making combination New England/Eastern Canada cruises. Noted visitors have included the *Westerdam*, the *Sagafjord*, the *Crystal Harmony* and the *Regent Sun*.

Canadian Pacific was for a time advertised as the world's largest transportation company. It operated a railroad (from Halifax some 3,500 miles across Canada to Vancouver), an airline, hotels, grain elevators, telegraph lines, ferries and a fleet of fine ocean-going ships. The *Empress of England* (opposite, top), shown arriving at Quebec City after a crossing from Liverpool and Greenock, was one of their largest Atlantic liners.

The Canadian Pacific freighter *Beavercove* (opposite), with the *Beaverdell* behind her, sailed in the 'ice free' months between Montreal, London, Liverpool and ports in Northern Europe. These cargo ships transported Canadian grain, timber, flour and - on seasonal occasions - Nova Scotian apples.
Canadian Pacific Steamships.

The Southampton Docks

Southampton was once called 'Britain's premier ocean liner port'. It played host to any number of great trans-Atlantic superliners – the *Queen Mary* and *Queen Elizabeth*, the *United States*, the *France* – and an even greater collection of smaller, but still well-known Holland America and North German Lloyd and P&O and Union-Castle liners. The list went on and on.

Southampton was at its most recent peak in the 1950s. Trans-Atlantic liners in particular came and went with almost daily regularity. There were the 'express ships', like the 'Mary' and the 'Elizabeth', that took five days to or from New York. When the brilliant *United States* arrived on her record-breaking maiden voyage in the summer of 1952, she crossed in 3½ days. But other ships took longer – nine days on the Dutch *Ryndam*, for example. There were also crossings available to Montreal and to Halifax and even to sunny Port Everglades.

Other liner services were more extensive, far more distant and exotic. The big P&O-Orient liners like the *Canberra* and the *Oriana* went out via the Suez Canal to Australia, then sometimes up to Hong Kong and Japan, and sometimes completely around-the-world in four or five months. The lavender-hulled Union-Castle liners sailed every Thursday afternoon with watch-setting regularity. Their destinations: Cape Town, Durban and other South African ports. The passenger-carrying 'banana boats' of the Fyffes Line (Britain's Chiquita fleet) sailed Caribbean waters, Royal Mail went to South America and the big, all-tourist class liners of the Shaw, Savill Line, the *Northern Star* and the *Southern Cross*, made regular 76-day circumnavigations.

The 1500-foot long Ocean Terminal, built in 1950 in classic, pre-War Art Deco style, was the most important and certainly most lavish passenger terminal. It had every convenience: lounges and waiting rooms and even train service direct to London. The Queens, the *France* and others like the *Nieuw Amsterdam* and the *Bremen* used it regularly. Most other liners used a long stretch of berths known as the Western Docks which handled cargo as well. There were speedy passenger connections to London's Waterloo Station by appropriately named 'boat trains', strings of specially arranged railway coaches that often bore the names of the shipping firms or steamers they served. These trains went directly alongside the ships themselves. There were also big drydocks in Southampton where ships like the mighty 83,000-ton *Queen Elizabeth*, the World's largest ocean liner, would go for their annual 'check-ups'.

But economics gradually cut deeper and deeper into Southampton's liner traffic. Airline competition, labor costs (and strikes) and the swing toward cruising from warm-weather ports led to the great decline. The grand old Ocean Terminal was, in fact, pulled down in 1983. The boat trains were gone as well. Southampton is still an important freight port with a massive, and expanding, container terminal, but the 'glory days' when it was one of the great liner capitals of the World have long since gone.

Southampton Docks: (opposite top) **The record breaking *United States* arrives, moving toward the Western Docks, while the Cunarders *Mauretania* and *Queen Mary* are in the background at the Ocean Terminal.** (opposite) **On another occasion, in February 1962, the world's longest liner, the 1,035-foot *France*, calls at the Ocean Terminal for the first time during her westbound maiden voyage to New York.** *Author's Collection.*

A large peacetime troop transport belonging to the Bibby Line of Liverpool, the 20,000-ton *Oxfordshire* had accommodations for 1,500 persons. She spent her days shuttling military personnel and their families to British bases and colonial outposts throughout the World. She is shown at Southampton Docks. When her trooping days were over she became the Sitmar Line's *Fairstar*, one of the most successful cruise ships in the Australian market. *Roger Sherlock.*

Liners at London

The Port of London was once the shipping capital of the World. Over 100 ships could be at the seemingly endless docks at any one time. Special sightseeing cruises were run just to look at them. And they seemed to be 'serenaded' by mighty flotillas of support craft: barges, tugs, floating derricks. The ships themselves represented the might and vast expanse of the old Empire. Evocatively named freighters and passenger liners came from all corners of the earth. There might be the *City of Madras* from Calcutta, the *Canberra Star* from Melbourne, the *Nowshera* from Zanzibar, the *Pacific Stronghold* from Vancouver. Big liners came to call as well – Cunard's *Saxonia* from Montreal, the *Amazon* from Rio, the *Durban Castle* from Mombasa and P&O's *Arcadia* from Sydney and Suva. These passenger ships actually had to follow an almost unique process. They would land their passengers and baggage down-river at the Tilbury Landing Stage, located about an hour's train ride from the heart of the Capital. Tugs would then shift the ships to the inner London freight docks, where they would offload their lucrative cargoes and then refill their holds with outward-bound merchandise. On leaving London there would be another short call at Tilbury to take on outward passengers.

But, as in most major world ports, the shipping business has changed drastically. Shifts in world politics and in trading patterns have dealt severe blows – far fewer ships and most of these under flags other than the Red Ensign. The Port of London grew very quiet, its pace almost silent, the docks in decay. But some parts of Docklands have taken on new roles – an airport, an office complex, a tourist centre. In other places along the twists and bends of the Thames, hints of the past remain: melancholy old warehouses, silent power stations, an abandoned shipyard.

Cruising from London seems to be thriving, however.

Vanished days of the great Port of London: Ellerman and British India freighters are among those being worked in this view of the Royal Albert Dock. *S.W. Rawlings.*

In another view, ships line both sides of the King George V Dock on a normal day in the 1950s. *S.W. Rawlings.*

The old Tilbury Landing Stage, first opened in 1930 and now restored as the London International Cruise Terminal, receives a steady parade of large ships, in summer mostly. In 1993, callers included the likes of the *Crystal Harmony*, the *Statendam* and the *Crown Odyssey*. Smaller cruiseships have an alternative. They can make their way further along the River, passing the new Queen Elizabeth II Bridge, the Thames Barrier and the old observatory and maritime museum at Greenwich. The famed Tower Bridge opens and they sail into the center of the City, to the so-called Pool of London. But instead of an actual terminal, ships such as the *Seabourn Pride*, the *Royal Viking Queen* and the *Song of Flower* moor alongside

a preserved Second World War warship, the *HMS Belfast*. Passengers cross her decks and then walk ashore, minutes away from Westminster and Piccadilly. In 1994 the Port of London handled more cruise passengers than any other British port, including Southampton. Further growth and development for London are expected.

And so, on a summer's evening in 1993, as we left the Tilbury Landing Stage on the 49,000-ton *Crystal Harmony*, we had to pause momentarily. The outbound *Enrico Costa* was already in the River, being readied by tugs for the run out into the North Sea. Upriver, the *Royal Viking Queen* was already underway. It was just another busy day for 'the liners at London'.

(opposite page) **In a closer view, foodstuffs are being offloaded from the United States Lines' *American Harvester* at London.** *Frank O. Braynard Collection.*

(right) **In another instance, in the Royal Albert Docks, Ellerman's *City of Carlisle* prepares to sail on her final voyage to the Far East in 1963. Typically of many British-flag freighters of that time, she was sold to 'overseas buyers' (in this case, the Greeks) before ending her days (in 1970) in an Eastern scrapyard.** *Cunard-Ellerman Group.*

Royal Occasion for the Royal Docks: Her Majesty Queen Elizabeth II, accompanied by Prince Philip, tours London's Royal Docks aboard the *St. Katherine* on May 12th 1959. Dressed in flags for the occasion, P&O's cargo liner *Ballarat* is at berth, offloading cargo from Australian ports such as Fremantle, Melbourne and Sydney. The officers, crew and guests cheered the Royal visitors as they sailed past on their inspection. Built in Scotland and delivered in July 1954, the 8,792-ton *Ballarat* did not carry passengers, unlike many similar freighters. *Frank O. Braynard Collection.*

A very rare visitor to London was the 11,000-ton Polish passenger ship *Sobieski*, which is shown moving outwards through the entrance lock at Tilbury Docks. She was built for the North Europe-South America service in 1939, but only a few months later was called to Allied war service. Released in 1946, she was returned to the Poles, who placed her on a special passenger run between Italy and New York. In 1950, she was taken by the Soviets and renamed *Gruzia*. Thereafter, she spent much of her life on the 'internal' Black Sea service. *S.W. Rawlings.*

The Liverpool Docks

In July 1990, a flash of the old days prevailed at Liverpool. The mighty *QE2* – on a celebratory cruise for Cunard's 150 years – called at the once-famous passenger port which for many years was Cunard's headquarters. Expectedly, the 963-foot long pride of the British merchant fleet drew tens of thousands. There were even gala fireworks.

Liverpool was once the second largest port in Britain and one of the busiest in all of Europe. Vast dockside warehouses were filled with sugar and tobacco, tea, cotton and salt. The great docks – with names like Huskisson, Canada, Princes, Salthouse and Brunswick – had welcomed some of the best known ships in the British merchant marine: Cunarders from New York and Montreal and Halifax, Pacific Steam Navigation's *Reina Del Mar* from Valparaiso, Booth Line's *Hubert* from Manaus, Elder Dempster's *Aureol* from Lagos, Anchor Line's *Caledonia* from Bombay, Blue Funnel's *Hector* from Sydney and Ellerman's *City of Cardiff* from Hong Kong. Princess Elizabeth (later the Queen) and Prince Philip returned from their Canadian tour aboard the *Empress of Scotland*, which reached Liverpool in November 1951.

"The docks were hectic with traffic back then," recalled Albert Stokes, a former Liverpudlian and keen harbor observer. "But after the vicious bombings by the Luftwaffe [a third of the City's buildings were either destroyed or damaged], we seemed never quite to recover. But if anything it was the 'end of Empire' that killed Liverpool as a port. The old trades disappeared and almost overnight. Then there were the Third World ships, the rise in container shipping and, of course, the shift by travellers from ocean liners to jet liners. I remember the last Cunard passenger sailing from Liverpool [the *Carinthia* in October 1967]. That seemed to be the end of it all."

But like many bygone port cities, Liverpool's waterfront is being revived – not for trade but for tourists. Several splendidly restored warehouses around the old Albert Dock now house the Merseyside Maritime Museum and a local branch of the Tate Gallery. The Maritime Museum is, of course, of particular fascination. It evokes the glorious past with ship models of all sizes, artifacts, maps, posters and special exhibitions. A retrieved propeller from the *Lusitania* (sunk in 1915) is now on display along with an enormous model of the equally ill-fated *Titanic*. It all sparks the spirit and heightens the imagination.

The liners at Liverpool: Three all-white Canadian Pacific Empress liners are shown in the Mersey. (opposite page) The *Empress of Britain* is docked at Princes Landing Stage, preparing for a regular crossing to Quebec City and Montreal. (right) The Company flagship, the 27,000-ton *Empress of Canada*, is ready to sail for Canada on one of her earliest voyages. (below) Finally, the veteran *Empress of France*, dating from 1928, is seen at anchor in the Mersey in 1960, her final year of service.
all photogaphs: F. Leonard Jackson.

Rotterdam: Europe's Busiest Port

"In the late 1940s, Rotterdam was recovering from the devastating damage of the Second World War. There was lots of rebuilding – new piers, new terminals, new warehouses, new rows of cranes," recalled Peter Houtmann, who worked as a clerk in the harborside offices of the Holland America Line. "But by the 1950s, Rotterdam had recovered and moved forward to become Europe's and later the World's busiest seaport. In those years, ocean ships seemed to be everywhere – rows of them at long quays, at anchorages, at shipyards and in what seemed to be a constant parade of ships coming and going."

By the late '50s, there were more than 21,000 calls by sea-going vessels at Rotterdam each year. In addition, there were some 200,000 arrivals by Rhine River and canal barges of all kinds. Other annual figures included over 4,000,000 tons of grain and 9,000,000 tons of ore. General cargo for 1959 amounted to 29,000,000 tons. Ships of almost every flag appeared in Rotterdam harbor.

"The beautiful passenger ships of the Holland America Line were, of course, well known. Many citizens of Rotterdam had some kind of direct contact with that Company and so their ships were looked upon as extensions of the City itself," remembered Mr. Houtmann. "The flagship *Nieuw Amsterdam* [built in 1938] was then the largest, the pride of the Netherlands and said to be one of the most magnificently decorated ships of her time. Together with the smaller *Maasdam*, the *Ryndam* and the new *Statendam* [1957], she sailed regularly to America, to New York via the Channel ports of Le Havre and Southampton. The combination liners *Noordam* and *Westerdam* ran a direct service to New York, sailing with year-round regularity every other Saturday. Then, with post-War American financial aid to Holland, the Company was able to build the magnificent *Rotterdam* in 1959. She was the first trans-Atlantic liner to dispense with the customary stack and instead she used twin uptakes. Built locally at the Rotterdam Dry Dock Company yard, she soon shared the beloved status that was held by the earlier *Nieuw Amsterdam*. And we also had the passenger ships of the Royal Rotterdam Lloyd – ships like the *Willem Ruys*, the *Sibajak* and the *Indrapoera* – that sailed to the East, to Indonesia and Australia."

"Of course, freighters were a large part of Rotterdam's activities," added Mr. Houtmann. "We had ships from the United States sailing for companies such as the United States Lines, the Black Diamond Line, the Meyer Line and the Waterman Line. The Lykes Line was noted for coming out of the U.S. Gulf. Of course, Holland America itself had a very large cargo fleet as well – Victory ships and C-3 type freighters received from the U.S. after the War and others like *Sommelsdyk*, the *Soestdyk* and the new 'K Class' of the 1950s with names like *Kerkedyk* and *Kinderdyk*. They carried Dutch products to the American East Coast and Gulf of Mexico ports, and these included cheeses, tulips and beer. There was also a North American West Coast service that passed through the Caribbean and the Panama Canal, and then called at ports such as Los Angeles, San Francisco, Seattle and Vancouver. For this, Holland America used combo ships such as the *Dinteldyk*, which could comfortably carry 50 or 60 passengers along with lots of freight."

Rotterdam had connections that served almost every continent. "The Rotterdam-South America Line, for example, sailed to the East Coast of South America, to ports like Rio and Buenos Aires," added Mr. Houtmann. "They too had combo ships with names like the *Alhena* and *Alnati*. They were large freighters, which also carried up to 50 or so passengers. Then there were the foreign companies. The likes of the Ellerman Line called en route to Africa, Blue Funnel and North German Lloyd to Southeast Asia and the NYK Line to the Orient."

Today, Rotterdam combined with nearby Europort handles some of the world's largest container ships, oil tankers and special cargo carriers. Expectedly, the inner harbor is much changed. Holland America's Wilhelminakade Terminal, for example, no longer handles ocean ships, but instead is rebuilt and restored as a hotel and restaurant. "When I returned to the City in the early 1980s," concluded Mr. Houtmann, "I was quite amazed to see how it had all changed. The activity, the great theatrical-like production of ship handling and ship movements, had vanished."

The *Nieuw Amsterdam*, for many years the flagship of the Holland America Line and one of the most popular trans-Atlantic liners, is seen at the Wilhelminakade Terminal, Rotterdam. *Holland America Line.*

(opposite page) **A heavy-lift crane loads Mercedes-Benz cars aboard a Mitsui Line freighter at Rotterdam. The date is the late 1950s.** *Frank O. Braynard Collection.*

Le Havre handled much of France's cargo trade as well as her passenger links. In this scene, the liners *Flandre* (left and on the New York run) and the *Colombie* (right and serving the Caribbean) are together at the Quai d'Escale.
Philippe Brebant Collection.

Antwerp's docks – 'the bustling port of all Belgium' – were dredged out of the low River Scheldt salt marshes six centuries before and had to be continually improved to handle the largest vessels. In this scene, at the Leopold Dock, one of the largest passenger-cargo liners on the colonial run to the Congo, the *Charlesville*, is at berth. A 10,900-ton ship built in 1951, she could carry considerable cargo as well as over 200 one-class passengers on her voyages to Lobito, Matadi and Boma. *Compagnie Maritime Belge.*

Hamburg handled about 750 vessels each month by the late 1950s. Inbound, ships delivered the likes of coal, coke and iron ore; outwards, they sailed with German manufactured goods such as automobiles, steel products and machinery. In this view, the Greek tramp *Hadiotis*, a Liberty ship, is offloading a cargo of grain from South America. An excursion steamer passes before her in the Elbe. In the background there is the giant Howaldtswerke shipyard. *Alvin E. Grant Collection.*

Bremerhaven was the most convenient German port for passenger ships, especially the trans-Atlantic liners. In this view from July 1959, the new North German Lloyd flagship *Bremen*, rebuilt from the French *Pasteur*, prepares to sail on her maiden voyage to New York. The liner *America* is just in front of her.

In the view on the right, a well-lighted *United States* remains overnight before beginning her next westbound crossing from Bremerhaven to New York via Le Havre and Southampton. *both photographs: Alvin E. Grant Collection.*

This aerial view at Lisbon shows four of Portugal's passenger liners on a rare occasion when they were in port together. Along the outer berths (from left to right) are the *Santa Maria* (serving the Caribbean and Florida) and the *Infante Dom Henrique* and *Vera Cruz* (both sailing to Portugese Africa). The fourth passenger ship, the smaller *Uige* (also in African service), is in drydock in the lower right. *Luis Miguel Correia Collection.*

(opposite page top) **Marseilles was France's busiest port in the South. Here, in this 1954 view, three passenger ships of Messageries Maritimes are at berth – the combo sisterships *Laos* and *Cambodge*, and then the passenger liner *Félix Roussel*. These ships sailed in Far East service, travelling out via the Suez Canal to over a dozen ports as far as Yokohama and Kobe.** *Eric Johnson Collection.*

(opposite page bottom) **Genoa, Italy's premier passenger port, received some of the world's greatest liners. In this view, the *Cristoforo Colombo* is to the left, pausing between voyages on her regular run to New York with calls at Naples, Cannes and Gibraltar. To the right, the Costa Line's *Federico C.* is about to sail for South America, carrying three classes of passengers to Rio, Santos, Montevideo and Buenos Aires.** *Everett Viez Collection.*

37

Smaller passenger and passenger-cargo ships traded on more localized services in Europe. Adriatica Line's *San Marco* sailed alternately from either Genoa and Naples or Trieste and Venice to Piraeus, Istanbul and Izmir. A motorship built in 1956, she could take 203 passengers – 92 in first class, 45 in second and 66 in tourist. *Alex Duncan.*

A former American passenger ship built in the early '30s, the *Istanbul* of the Turkish Maritime Lines provided a link that was similar to that of the *San Marco* except that she also called at Marseilles and Barcelona. *Roger Sherlock.*

The Soviet *Ukraina*, built for Rumanian owners in 1938, sailed in the Black Sea. Along with a number of other passenger ships, she traded on the 'Express Line' between Odessa, Eupatoria, Yalta, Novorossisk, Tuapse, Sochi, Sukhumi, Poti and Batumi. A 640-passenger ship, she also ran occasional extended trips to Lebanon and Egypt, and some cruises. She is shown while berthed at Valletta on Malta. *Michael Cassar.*

Finally, in Northern waters, the Swedish Lloyd Line's *Saga* sailed across the North Sea between London and Gothenburg. Built in 1946, this smart-looking 6,500-tonner was sold a decade later to the French and became the *Ville De Bordeaux* for Marseilles-Corsica service. *Swedish Lloyd.*

The North Atlantic was noted by many as the most treacherous of seas. Winter storms were especially feared. In this scene, a Holland America Line freighter has arrived at Hoboken, New Jersey covered in thick ice after a January crossing from Rotterdam and Antwerp. *Moran Towing & Transportation Company.*

Chapter Two
Tropical Waters
The Caribbean and South America

The Grace Line to Latin America

In 1945-46, as the Second World War ended and commercial services resumed in full force, the New York-based Grace Line – much like almost all other major shipowners – ordered new ships. They planned over a dozen 12-passenger freighters as well as nine specially designed combo liners which could take up to 52 passengers each in quarters that were then amongst the most modern afloat. On this *Santa Maria* class, for example, every stateroom had a private bathroom, the dining room was air-conditioned, there was an outdoor pool and even an outdoor movie screen which was attached to the cross-tree mast for after-dinner screenings under tropic stars. Three of the ships sailed in regular 18-day roundtrip Caribbean service; the other six worked a 40-day schedule via the Panama Canal and then along almost the entire length of the West Coast of South America.

Founded back in 1892, W. R. Grace & Company began in the South American trades with steamships that rounded Cape Horn on their trips out of New York. The voyage all the way to Valparaiso then took approximately 38 days, a great improvement over the 100 or so days needed by the earlier sailing ships. After the opening of the Panama Canal in 1914, the service took less than a fortnight and regularities increased. By the 1930s, the Grace Line was one of the most important carriers under the US-flag and had a well-regarded fleet that included four brand new passenger liners, which sailed both from the US East Coast and from the West Coast.

By the 1950s, there were four Grace Line sailings every Friday afternoon from New York. One of the twin-funnel passenger liners, either the *Santa Rosa* or the *Santa Paula*, often led this procession. They were off on 12-day cruises to Curacao, La Guaira, Puerto Cabello and Cartagena. Then, one of the 52-passenger ships, perhaps the *Santa Sofia*, followed on an 18-day voyage to Puerto Cabello, Amuay Bay, Maracaibo and Barranquilla. A second 52-passenger combo ship, possibly the *Santa Margarita*, followed next. Her 40-or-so-day itinerary took her to Cristobal, the Panama Canal, Balboa, Buenaventura, Guayaquil, Telara (Peru), Callao, Mollendo (Peru), Arica (Chile), Antofagasta, Chanaral and eventually Valparaiso. Finally, one of the 12-passenger freighters might follow, bound for Curacao, Maracaibo, La Salina, Lagunillas, Amuay Bay, La Guaira, Puerto Cabello, Puerto la Cruz, Guanta, Cumana and Carupano.

In 1970 and in the face of declining profits for US shipowners, Grace was merged with the Prudential Lines and, for a time, traded as the Prudential-Grace Lines before losing its identity altogether. Presently, the W .R. Grace Company is a huge petrochemicals giant far removed from the sea and shipping.

(opposite top) **While they continued to be registered at San Francisco until the very end of their Grace Line sailing days in 1958, the twin sisters *Santa Paula* (just sailing) and the *Santa Rosa* were well-known to New York harbor-watchers. One of them sailed every Friday at noon, bound for a 12-day cruise to the Caribbean. In this instance, with both ships together at Manhattan's Piers 57 and 58, their schedules have been disrupted by an American seamen's strike. Both ships were sold to Typaldos Lines of Greece and endured years of idleness after that company went bankrupt. The former *Santa Rosa*, however, eventually enjoyed a brief period of stardom, playing the part of the *Titanic* in a film.** *Everett Viez Collection.*

(opposite) **Grace Line's modified C2-Class passenger-cargo combination ship *Santa Maria* sails from New York's Pier 58 on her maiden voyage on the 31st August, 1946. A very modern-looking ship for that time, she is outward bound for the West Coast of South America. She and her five identical sisters operated a weekly sailing on a six-week turnaround basis. Southward, the *Santa Maria* and her sisters carried a wide variety of U.S. goods including autos, iron and steel products, machinery, glass, clothing and chemicals. Northbound, she would carry fruit, vegetables, hides, copper and pig iron from Chile; tin, antimony, wolfram and zinc from Bolivia; bananas, balsa wood and cocoa beans from Ecuador; coffee and platinum from Colombia; and frozen shrimps and hardwoods from the Canal Zone.** *Frank O. Braynard Collection.*

Migration to and from the Caribbean peaked in the late 1950s and early '60s. Europeans, especially Italians, Spaniards and Portugese, were seeking new lives with better opportunity in Venezuela while, in reverse, Jamaicans and other West Indians were settling in Britain. Many ships, such as the Italian-flag *Irpinia*, a 13,600-ton passenger ship owned by Grimaldi-Siosa Lines, catered for migrants in both directions. She is seen arriving at Miami on a special call in the summer of 1959. *James L. Shaw Collection.*

(opposite top left) **The French Line's passenger service to the West Indies was justified, like so many other passenger and cargo trades, by colonial links. The ships sailed to both Guadeloupe and Martinique in the Caribbean as well as nearby French Guiana on continental South America. One of the finest ships in this service was the 13,800-ton** *Colombie*, **completed in 1931. Built in the high-spirited era of such ships as the** *Ile De France*, **the** *Champlain* **and, possibly the most magnificent of all, the** *Normandie*, **the 509-foot long** *Colombie* **was in many ways a miniature version of these larger ships. Her accommodations, including a descending stairwell into her fist class restaurant, a noted French Line feature, reflected the glories of the Art Deco era at sea. The** *Colombie* **is seen here, in an aerial view of Pointe-à-Pitre on Guadeloupe, together with a French Line Liberty ship.** *Philippe Brebant Collection.*

(opposite top right) **The French Line also employed a fleet of white-hulled 'banana boats' on their Caribbean service as well as some breakbulk freighters such as the 7,600-ton** *Equateur*. **Shown while on a special call at Miami, she was then sailing between Le Havre, the Caribbean and ports in the Gulf of Mexico.** *Frank O. Braynard Collection.*

(opposite) **An especially splendid-looking liner, the 20,000-ton** *Antilles* **was built in 1953 particularly for the French Line's Caribbean service. While shown at New Orleans during a special cruise call there, she was normally routed from Le Havre, Southampton and Vigo (in northern Spain) to San Juan, Pointe-à-Pitre, Fort de France, La Guaira, Trinidad and Barbados. Her sistership, the** *Flandre*, **which sailed out to New York from spring until fall, assisted on this tropic service in winter. Three-class ships, both were later victims of ruinous fires: the** *Antilles* **being lost in the Caribbean in 1971, the former** *Flandre* **in Greek waters in 1994.** *Eric Johnson Collection.*

The United Fruit 'Banana Boats'

They were like elegant white yachts. They had classic lines – a graceful rake, tall brown masts, traditional sterns, extended superstructures and distinctively painted stacks. Except for a handful of mostly breakbulk freighters (like the C1-type *Cape Ann* class), they were painted completely in white. Straight off the pages of romantic fiction, they were known as 'banana boats'. They even had romantic sounding names – *Comayagua* and *Heredia*, *Cibao* and *Morazan*, *Antigua* and *Veragua*. They were familiar sights in many American ports: New York, Boston, Baltimore, New Orleans, Los Angeles. Busily, they sailed with general freight mostly to the Caribbean, Central America and sometimes farther afield to South America, and then returned with their most prized cargo. In 1955, the United Fruit Company delivered over 43,000,000 stems of bananas to the United States.

Following losses in the Second World War and amidst other changes in their operations, the Company revived six of their 99-passenger combination liners in the late '40s. The *Talamanca*, *Veragua* and *Jamaica* handled the New York service, sailing on 17-day roundtrips to Havana, Puerto Cortez (in Honduras) and Puerto Barrois (Guatemala). The full cruise was priced from $340 in 1950. The *Antigua* and *Quirigua* sailed from New Orleans to Havana and Puerto Barrois while the *Chiriqui* sailed from that same Louisiana port but to Cristobal and Puerto Barrois. Built in 1932-33, these ships were, however, downgraded to all-freight status by the mid-'50s. Air competition, increased operational costs and a shift in Company policy prompted this decision and later led to the transfer and sale of these same ships for foreign-flag service. Some went to Elders & Fyffes, the British subsidiary of United Fruit.

The Company's most notable new ships were the 1945-47 built *Fra Berlanga* class. Handsome ships of 7,000 gross tons and 455 feet in length, the others were named *Comayagua*, *Esparta*, *Heredia*, *Junior*, *Limon*, *Metapan*, *Parismina* and *San Jose*. Along with a dozen passengers in very attractive quarters (with air-conditioning which was an extension of the ships' vast cooling systems) they could carry in their four holds up to 78,000 stems of bananas. Similar looking, but smaller versions of these ships were built in 1947-48. At 5,000 tons, the *Yaque* class consisted of nine sisterships, with the others being the *Cibao*, *Hibueras*, *Morazan*, *Quisqueya*, *Santa Cerro*, *Sixoala*, *Tivives* and *Ulua*. In total, these ships and the others steamed 5 million nautical miles a year.

At the very beginning of the lower Hudson River piers at New York, there was a huge, illuminated sign at the far end of one. Jutting some 600 feet into the River waters, it read 'The Great White Fleet'. Often, three or four 'Fruitco' ships were at these docks together, resting in the shadows of the great office towers of Lower Manhattan and often being readied for Friday departures. Inbound, the ship almost always went farther upriver to a special berth, the 'banana exchange' terminal, at Weehawken, New Jersey. Distinctive for its tall banana-offloading crane-conveyors, it was located just across from the slips of 'Luxury Liner Row'. Two ships at once could be handled, offloading their cooled cargoes into refrigerator trucks and railway cars. The process might take 2-3 days. The empty ships would then be shifted by tugs to one of the Lower New York City piers, where they would load general cargo for tropical destinations. There were three or four sailings a week in the early 1950s as shown by this sample schedule:

Fri Apr 6	*Talamanca*
Fri Apr 6	*Heredia*
Fri Apr 6	*Tivives*
Fri Apr 6	*Cape May*
Thu Apr 12	*Toltec*
Fri Apr 13	*Esparta*
Fri Apr 13	*Veragua*
Fri Apr 13	*Choluteca*

By the 1960s, United Fruit was also using many Dutch-flag 'banana boats' of the Caraibische Scheepvaart Maats., which was managed by the well-known firm of Van Nievelt, Goudriaan & Company. Ships such as the *Cartago* and *Turrialba* ran in US-Caribbean service. But the fleet was gradually reduced, primarily due to the escalating costs of operating American-flag ships and because of increasing foreign-flag competition. After US Government charter sailings to transport military supplies out to troubled Southeast Asia, the sisterships of the *Fra Berlanga* and the *Yaque* classes were transferred to the British and Dutch flags before going to the breakers by the mid-1970s. By this time, United Fruit was reliant on foreign-flag, chartered tonnage. Other changes included the replacement of New York, for example, by the port of Albany, 140 miles northward on the Hudson, which was seen for a time as a more efficient distribution point for the American Northeast. This has since been changed as well. The Company name became United Brands and today it runs a small fleet of chartered ships.

(opposite page) **The combination liner *Quirigua* approaches the dock at Puerto Cortez, where she will land general cargo from New Orleans and nearly 100 passengers. But with changes, her superstructure was cutdown in 1953 and her 99 passenger berths eliminated. (above) In her rebuilt state, she is shown arriving at New York, about to be docked at United Fruit's 'banana exchange' terminal at Weehawken, New Jersey.**
Frank O. Braynard Collection.

A moodful setting: the *San Jose* sits amongst the natural splendor of Golfito, a port on the west coast of Costa Rica. She had been completed in June, 1945 by the Gulf Shipbuilding Corporation of Chickasaw, Alabama, one of nine identical sisters. Later, she suffered not one but two mishaps. In November, 1967, while under charter to the U.S. Government, she caught fire while bound from Guam to Vietnam. Ships raced to the scene and an American destroyer attempted a tow back to port, but the towline soon parted and the 455-foot long ship was abandoned. She drifted with the fire spreading rapidly. Later, she was sighted during an air search and subsequently a U.S. Navy LST found her stable and with no sign of fire. Towed back to Guam by a tug, she was placed alongside a berth and cargo discharge commenced, but when her fore hatches were opened, fire broke out afresh. Shifted from her berth she was deliberately grounded and the fore holds flooded. Surveys showed her to be badly damaged, with buckled plating and gutted accommodations. She was towed, however, in March, 1968 to a Seattle shipyard and repaired fully. In 1970 she joined Elders & Fyffes, went under the British flag and was renamed *Ronde*. But in January, 1972 she stranded on beach at Tela in Honduras. She was refloated and later towed to Galveston for repairs. The ship was scrapped on Taiwan in 1976. *Frank O. Braynard Collection.*

Elders & Fyffes Limited were Britain's best known 'banana boat' firm. A subsidiary of the United Fruit Company, they had a fleet of their own, but also inherited several of their American 'cousins'. Three of United Fruit's 1932-33 built 'express passenger-mail ships', the *Talamanca*, *Veragua* and *Quirigua*, were transferred

to London registry. Having been already reduced to all-freighter status, they sailed between UK ports, Rotterdam and the Caribbean as the *Sulaco*, *Sinaloa* (shown in the London Docks) and *Samala*. The former, aft passenger spaces (including the original outdoor swimming pools) had become additional cargo space. In total, they could carry up to 150,000 stems of bananas. But as newer, more competitive 'reefers' (refrigerated ships) came into service, often from foreign-flag competitors, these thirty-year veterans finally went to the breakers. The *Sinaloa* finished her days in 1964 at Bruges in Belgium. *Steffen Weirauch Collection.*

Port Everglades

When Florida's Port Everglades first opened for business back in 1926, it was a sleepy oil tanker port. Then there were no luxury liners, no cruise terminals and certainly no nearby airport at Fort Lauderdale. But by the late 1950s as cruise lines were looking for alternatives (to New York mostly) for their winter Caribbean cruises, geographically well-suited Port Everglades (along with Miami, which is some 20 miles south) took root.

"Costa Line's little *Franca C.* was our first winter season cruiseship. She first arrived here in December 1959," according to Robert Pelletier, Customer Relations Manager at the Port Everglades Authority and himself a passenger ship historian. "A great success, she was followed by larger ships, the *Bianca C.* and the *Anna C.* Grace Line came every week with their *Santa Rosa* and *Santa Paula*, which called here as part of their 13-day cruises from New York. We also had one regular trans-Atlantic service. Portugal's 20,000-ton *Santa Maria* (there was also a Grace liner of the same name at that time) ran a year-round service to and from Lisbon, Madeira, the Canary Islands and several Caribbean ports."

"The number of winter cruiseship callers soon increased. Pier space was needed and so we often had to use a temporary facility at a cargo terminal. By the 1960s, we had the likes of the Home Lines, Furness-Bermuda, Cunard and Moore-McCormack. Some ships called at the beginning of long, luxurious trips. These included Cunard's *Caronia*, Swedish American's *Gripsholm* and *Kungsholm*, and Norwegian America's *Bergensfjord* and *Oslofjord*," according to Pelletier. "And we also had many ships from those pre-jet, long-distance liner services. There were the Royal Rotterdam Lloyd, P&O-Orient Lines, the New Zealand Shipping Company, Chandris, the Shaw Savill Line, American President and the Orient Overseas Line. P&O's big *Canberra* might have sailed from England all the way to Australia and then up to the North American West Coast before passing through Panama and then calling at Port Everglades en route home to the UK. The Dutch liner *Willem Ruys* might call on a voyage from Rotterdam to Sydney via Florida and Panama."

Presently, Port Everglades has a dozen passenger ship berths, which include docks for such 'day cruisers' as *Discovery Dawn*. And while the future will bring such ships as the 104,000-ton *Grand Princess* (1998), business is booming even now. Nearly a third of the Port's resources are for cruiseships and, in December, 1996, a record-breaking 11 liners were in port together. This 'armada' consisted of the *Sun Princess*, *Golden Princess*, *Century*, *Cunard Dynasty*, *Ryndam*, *Westerdam*, *Rotterdam*, *Royal Odyssey*, *Silver Cloud*, *Norwegian Crown* and *Galaxy*. On the following day 8 cruiseships were together – the *QE2*, *Ryndam*, *Veendam*, *Crystal Symphony*, *Dreamward*, *Star Princess*, *Costa Victoria* and *Costa Romantica*. Unquestionably, Port Everglades is a cruiseship capital!

The Portugese liner *Santa Maria* was a regular caller at Port Everglades from 1956 until 1973. Built at the Cockerill-Ougrée shipyard in Hoboken, Belgium in 1953, the 609-foot long *Santa Maria* had originally been used on the Lisbon-Rio de Janeiro-Santos service and carried no less than four classes of passengers. On January 22nd, 1961 the 20,906-ton ship made worldwide headlines when, while sailing from Curacao to Port Everglades, she was hijacked by armed rebels opposed to the Salazar regime in Portugal. They took control of the liner, cut radio contact with the outside world and set course for Angola. The ship was first sighted on the 25th. On the 28th, after protracted radio negotiations, the rebels agreed to sail to Brazil and release the 600 passengers. She arrived at Recife on the 2nd February, disembarked her worried guests and was then set to sail for Africa. But the harbor was blocked by warships and the ship's crew staged a sit-down strike. The rebels surrendered and the ship was returned to her owners, Companhia Colonial of Lisbon. *William Rau Collection.*

American Cruising: Winter 1962-63

Thomas Cook used to issue regular booklets listing each and every cruise and trans-Atlantic sailing for the next six or eight months. Odd pages even mentioned trans-Pacific voyages, cruises from places like New Orleans and San Francisco, and the novelty (in about a half page) of short cruises out of Miami and Port Everglades. In all, some 75 passenger ships representing 30 steamship firms were listed. I have several dozen of these booklets in my files and recently I looked over the one for winter 1962-63.

In the cruise section, the Christmas-New Year's list was most impressive, although 95% of the sailings were out of New York. Eleven days to the Caribbean on Cunard's grand old second *Mauretania* could cost $330; 14 days on the superb *Gripsholm* started at $450; and 17 days on the Moore-McCormack *Argentina* was priced from $560. There were also shorter, less expensive trips: 5 days to Bermuda on the *America* ($160), 6 days on the *Ocean Monarch* ($130) and a week to Nassau on Home Lines' *Italia* ($170). Extended holiday cruises included a 23-day run to the western Mediterranean aboard the *Independence* ($475 in cabin class and up), 26 days to the Panama Canal, Peru and Ecuador on the *Santa Maria* ($800) and 31 days to the East Coast of South America, including Rio and Buenos Aires, on the *Brasil* (from $1100).

The list of 'Long Cruises' filled several pages of their own and ranged from 60 days to the Mediterranean on Zim Lines' little *Jerusalem* (from $1600) to 80 days around-the-world on the Dutch flagship *Rotterdam* (from $2700). Only two ships went completely around-the-world that year: the *Rotterdam* and Cunard's *Caronia*. Two (the *Bergensfjord* and the *Kungsholm*) went all around the Pacific, another (the *Gripsholm*) encircled continental South America, one (the *Argentina*) did a combination of South America and Africa, and then no less than 7 ships did long, mid-winter Mediterranean cruises from New York (the *Olympia*, *Mauretania*, *Oslofjord*, *Leonardo Da Vinci*, *Empress Of Canada*, *Gripsholm* and the *Independence*).

Florida had a very small listing in those days, showing the likes of a 2-day trip from Miami to Nassau and back on Costa's *Franca C.* for $45 and 7 days to the western Caribbean on Eastern's *Evangeline* for $160. The West Coast schedules included 10 days to Hawaii and back on the *Lurline*; the South Seas and Australia on another Matson liner, the *Mariposa*; and a six-week cruise all the way to England but via Singapore and India and the Suez Canal on P&Os *Himalaya*.

What a keepsake, what a selection – I only wish I could call Cook's in the morning!

Formerly Furness-Bermuda Line's *Monarch of Bermuda* of 1931, the greatly rebuilt *Arkadia*, then sailing for the Greek Line, ran Caribbean cruises from a chilly New York in the winter of 1959. Shown at Pier 88 in an ice-filled Hudson River, she had the novelty of a dipod mast which served as an additional funnel. While used for about 9 months of the year in North Atlantic service between Northern Europe and Eastern Canada, she later cruised from Southampton to Spain, Portugal, West Africa and the Atlantic islands.
John Gillespie Collection.

The Argentine merchant fleet grew significantly after the Second World War. Cargo ships were acquired from the United States and a series of brand new passenger ships were built abroad. In this aerial view from 1951, the 116-passenger combination liner *Rio Jachal* arrives at New York on her maiden voyage from Buenos Aires. Built at Genoa, she and her two sisterships ran a six-week roundtrip service to ports along the East Coast of South America. *Frank O. Braynard Collection.*

For the service between Buenos Aires and London, the Argentinians had three combo sisters, including the *Libertad* which carried 96 first class-only passengers in great comfort. *Schiffsfotos Jansen.*

The Argentinian fleet also included specialized passenger ships for the busy migrant trades, both from Northern Europe and from the Mediterranean. This group included the converted Victory ship *Cordoba*, which was refitted to carry 800 third class passengers. Shown at Hamburg, she had been the *NYU Victory*, built in 1945. *Schiffsfotos Jansen.*

New Orleans, the largest and busiest port in the US Gulf, was home to the Lykes Lines. One of America's biggest shipowners in the years following the Second World War, they ran services to almost every continent. In this view, from the early 1950s, the C2-type freighter *Helen Lykes* heads off for the Mediterranean. *Frank O. Braynard Collection.*

The Alcoa Steamship Company was the transport division of the giant Aluminium Company of America (Alcoa was their acronym). Their ships were, in fact, painted in distinctive bright silver and light grey to emphasise their products. Strongly linked to the Caribbean and the northeast coast of South America, their fleet in the 1950s included a series of C1-Class cargo ships such as the 12-passenger *Alcoa Puritan* (shown arriving at New York and being assisted by a McAllister Towing Company tug). Timed to regular schedules, Alcoa offered services from New York, New Orleans, Mobile and Montreal (or Halifax in winter). The 30-day cruises from Eastern Canada, for example, were routed to Bermuda, St Kitts, Antigua, St Lucia, Barbados, St Vincent, Grenada, Trinidad and Georgetown. Built during the Second World War, in 1943, at Wilmington, California, the *Alcoa Puritan* sailed until 1963, when she joined the U.S. Government's 'mothball fleet.' But two years later, she was declared surplus and went to shipbreakers at Mobile, Alabama.
Alcoa Steamship Company.

Moore-McCormack to South America

The New York-based Moore-McCormack Lines were one of the major carriers in the South American trade in the 1950s. Their fleet of over two dozen ships traded to East Coast ports – in Brazil, Uruguay and Argentina – and mostly from U.S. East Coast ports. There was a second service however, from the American West Coast via Panama. The Company also had two subsidiaries, the American Scantic Line to Scandinavian ports and the Robin Line to South and East Africa. In this view, the C3-type freighter *Mormacmar* is taking on heavy cargo. Being loaded with the assistance of a floating crane, it is bound for Bahia in Brazil. *Frank O. Braynard Collection.*

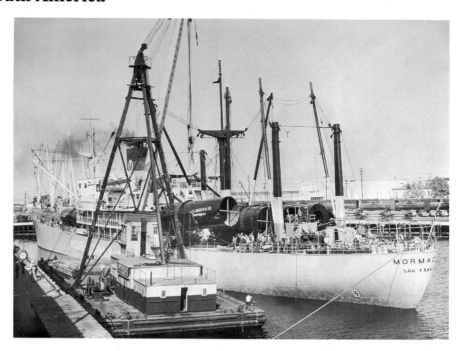

South America Bound: At least two floating cranes are alongside Moore-McCormack's *Mormacelm* as she loads at New York's Pier 32. She has taken on heavy machinery bound for Brazilian ports: Recife, Fortaleza, Rio and Santos. The *Mormacelm* was one of more than 400 standardized Victory ships built in the last years of the Second World War. These Victory cargo ships were faster than the Liberty types; steam turbine power gave them a 17-knot service speed against the Liberty's 11. Other characteristics of the Victory were the long forecastle and the high deckhouse. Completed in July 1945 as the *Coffeyville Victory*, the 455-foot long ship was transferred to Moore-McCormack and sailed for them until scrapped at Hong Kong in 1970. *Moore-McCormack Lines.*

(opposite page) The Erie Railroad tug *Paterson* has just delivered boxed freight to the Moore-McCormack liner *Argentina* at New York. She and two sisters, the *Brazil* and the *Uruguay*, ran a 38-day roundtrip service to Trinidad, Rio de Janeiro, Santos, Montevideo and Buenos Aires. The passenger trade was balanced between one-way, port-to-port traffic and roundtrip cruise travellers. *Erie Railroad.*

Little Dutch ships with Greek names might be a brief way of describing the vast fleet of KNSM, known to the English-speaking world as the Royal Netherlands Steamship Company. Small freighters such as the engines-aft *Adonis* carried 3-12 passengers on month-long voyages from Amsterdam, New York and from US Gulf ports to Port au Prince, Ciudad Trujillo, Aruba, Curacao, Maracaibo, Puerto Cabello, La Guaira, Trinidad, Demerara and Paramaribo. *Royal Netherlands Steamship Company.*

The latest addition to the Grancolombiana fleet (Flota Mercante Grancolombiana) was the streamlined *Ciudad De Quito*, photographed on her maiden arrival at New York on December 1st 1949. Built by Canadian Vickers Ltd and powered by a Norberg diesel, she was one of a series of new ships that went into service from Canadian, US East Coast and US Gulf ports to Colombian and Ecuadorean ports. Outwards, she was supported by cargoes of American manufactured goods; inward to New York, she carried large amounts of coffee and bananas. *Frank O. Braynard Collection.*

In a similar service, the Venezuelan Line ran several freighters such as the 12-passenger *Merida* on a weekly service between New York, other US East Coast ports and La Guaira, Barranquilla and Maracaibo.

Frank O. Braynard Collection.

The C1-M class of wartime-built American freighters were amongst the smallest mass-produced ships. They measured 3,800 gross tons, were 338 feet in length and had a width of 50 feet. They carried a crew of 35 and could make 11 knots at best. Typically, many found further life under foreign flags after the Second World War. Completed in October 1945, the *Crown Knot* was sold to Peruvian owners in 1947 and became their *Huallaga*. For some time thereafter she was used in regular service from New York to Havana, Cristobal, Guayaquil, Callao, Arica, Antofagasta and Valparaiso. Sold to other South American interests in 1969 and renamed *Pan De Azucar*, she had an unfortunate end. Seized by the Ecuadorean authorities at Guayaquil in January 1974, she caught fire shortly afterward and then was beached to avoid sinking. Heavily damaged, she later began to list, then sank with only her masts and bridge deck above the water.

Frank O. Braynard Collection.

Visit to Rio

Even though it was early winter in Brazil, a summer-like haze hung over Guanabara Bay. The great Niteroi Bridge was almost lost in the yellowed mists. While the port of Rio de Janeiro is not the largest or even the busiest along the East Coast of South America (in fact, those titles belong to another Brazilian port: Santos, the bustling harbor for Sao Paulo), it is certainly the most romantic. Shipping was, of course, the seed from which sprang the growth of the city, today perhaps best-known for Sugar Loaf and the High Christ and those fabled beaches of Copacabana and Ipanema.

It was a Sunday morning, but the port could not have been more active – two dozen ships were officially 'listed'. There were French and Italian freighters, great Chinese bulk carriers and oil tankers flying the colors of Liberia and Panama and, less expectedly, Bulgaria. The local shipyard stood across the bay, a string of those stork-like container cranes worked a row of ships and, in a far-off corner, six or so freighters were nested together, all of them out of work as a result of the bankruptcy of the national shipowner, Lloyd Brasileiro. But, amidst it all, my immediate attention centered on the Ocean Passenger Terminal. Looked after by a single stevedore, I was the lone passenger awaiting the mid-day arrival of the container liner *Americana*. She would take me northwards to New York. But during my wait, it was all so easy to drift back in time, to the days when Rio was a booming ocean liner port, in the final era before the determined inroads of the airlines.

Well into the 1960s, as many as a half dozen passenger ships might line Rio's docks at any one time. Mostly, these ships were on 'line voyages', to other ports along the East Coast as far south as Buenos Aires and then north to New York and New Orleans, London and Hamburg, Lisbon and Naples, and – in the extreme – over to Cape Town and then to very distant Singapore and Hong Kong. These were the global passenger ship links, vessels which relied as much on their class-divided passengers (from opulent, upper-deck first class to spartan, below-deck steerage) as they did on their precious cargoes: the manufactured goods, the heavy machinery, the leather shoes and textiles, the cashew nuts and – perhaps most valuable – the huge consignments of coffee. Their passenger rosters then included far less tourists, but the corporate people, the clergy, the students and the last masses of southern European immigrants seeking new lives in the cities and Latin American interior.

The best known liners to call at Rio in those days were the last of the old 'Good Neighbor Fleet', Moore-McCormack's *Argentina* and *Brasil*. Big and luxurious and superbly run, they sailed to New York. Competition on the same route, with generally two calls at Rio per trip, one southbound and the other north, came from an Argentine trio: the *Rio De La Plata*, *Rio Jachal* and *Rio Tunuyan*. To New Orleans, there were the three splendid ships of the Delta Line – the *Del Mar*, *Del Norte* and *Del Sud*.

Combo liners, with fancy first class quarters and sometimes with less expensive, less spacious accommodations in tourist, dominated the North European services. Too numerous to mention all, there were the likes of the three sisters of the *Amazon* class of Britain's Royal Mail Lines (they advertised 15 days from London to Rio), a quartet from the Blue Star Line and another trio flying the Argentine colors. The French ran ships such as the *Pasteur* and the *Louis Lumière*, and then there were the Hamburg-South American Line, the Rotterdam South America Line and Sweden's Johnson Line.

Mediterranean services to Rio tended to be even more class-divided: luxurious first class, a similar but more economical cabin class and then, most profitable, a large-capacity third class. The Italian Line ran several splendid liners including the well-remembered *Augustus* and *Giulio Cesare*. And long before it went so deeply into cruising, the Costa Line ran three-class ships as well, most of them secondhand conversions. The French had the *Bretagne* and the *Provence* out of Marseilles, Spain was represented by the Ybarra Line and Portugal had their big, 21,000-ton sisterships *Santa Maria* and *Vera Cruz*. Lastly, and almost unique in the annals of passenger shipping, Holland's Royal Interocean Lines ran no less than 5 passenger ships that, in fact, never went near Amsterdam. Instead, they worked a very ambitious 5-month schedule that began at Rio and other South American ports before crossing over to South and East Africa, Southeast Asia and then up to Hong Kong and Japan. A full roundtrip meant a voyage of 160 days or more.

Today, Rio's passenger ship traffic is busiest between December and March, high summer in South America. Cruiseships call on coastal voyages, on Amazon River trips and on runs down to Antarctica.

Finally, the container-filled *Americana* appeared and then went to her berth on that humid June afternoon. As I readied myself to go aboard, I had one last thought of Rio's Ocean Terminal and the fine ships which once used it.

Among the liners trading to the East Coast of South America in the 1950s were Royal Mail Lines' *Highland Chieftain*, which sailed from London, Vigo, Lisbon and Las Palmas. A large combination passenger-cargo liner, she had special refrigerated spaces to bring home Argentine beef. She could also carry some 100 passengers in first class and another 330 in third class. *Royal Mail Lines.*

Far more reliant on passengers was Italy's Costa Line with ships such as the *Anna C.* Formerly Furness Withy's *Southern Prince* of 1929, she had been rebuilt after the Second World War, in 1948, to carry as many as 337 first class and 664 third class passengers on regular runs from Genoa and Naples across to Rio, Santos, Montevideo and Buenos Aires. *Costa Line.*

The largest post-War French liners on the South American run were the near-sisters *Provence* (pictured) and *Bretagne.* Completed in 1951-52 for the Marseilles-based Société Général de Transports Maritimes, they had a wide range of passenger accommodations, which onboard the 1,302-passenger *Provence*, ranged from deluxe suites in first class to large dormitories in third class. For about ten years, this pair was routed from Marseilles, Genoa, Naples and Barcelona to Dakar, Bahia, Rio de Janeiro, Santos, Montevideo and Buenos Aires. But by the early 1960s, with declining loads on the South American passenger run, both ships turned to cruising. *Transports Maritimes.*

Cargo handling at Rio: stevedores load coffee aboard Moore-McCormack Lines' *Mormacsea*.
Peter Lancaric Collection.

Chapter Three
The African Trades

The ports had names like Mombasa and Mtwara, Beira and Dar-es-Salaam. The wharves were bustling and crowded, often backlogged and crammed with cargoes such as cloves and cashew nuts, coffee and sisal. Hans Andresen, a chemical engineer, and his wife Jule, having been residents of East Africa for over thirty years, are great devotees of passenger ship travel. Their record is impressive: they have travelled to date on over 200 different ships. Recently, in the superb comfort of the Queens Grill Lounge onboard a westbound *Queen Elizabeth 2*, they recalled some of their ocean travels. According to Mr. Andresen, "We have always avoided air travel wherever possible. We have kept abreast of almost all the shipping schedules and even those special, once-a-year sailings." To this Mrs. Andresen added, "My father was a Chief Justice in British colonial East Africa and we travelled, beginning in the 'thirties – but excepting the War years – at least once but sometimes twice a year from Britain. I sailed in almost all the Union-Castle liners, beginning with the old *Llangibby Castle*. Often, we sailed from Durban by way of East London, Port Elizabeth and Cape Town to Southampton. I especially recall liners like the *Arundel Castle* and *Capetown Castle*, the *Athlone Castle* and the *Pretoria Castle*. Many years later, in August 1977, it somehow seemed rather appropriate that we should be on the final Union-Castle sailing, in the *Windsor Castle*. This was the very end of regular Union-Castle service to and from Africa. Never again would there be that precise and continual convenience. The *Windsor Castle* was a wonderful ship, with lovely first class accommodations. Onboard that final northbound trip, there were many nostalgic passengers, people who had been travelling on the Castle liners for years and years. I also recall lots of Rhodesians, all of them returning to Britain."

In the 1950s and 1960s Mr. and Mrs. Andresen literally 'commuted' between Britain and East Africa. "Mostly, we'd use the British India Line out of London, taking either their *Kenya* or *Uganda*, to Port Said, the Suez Canal, Aden, Mombasa, Tanga, Zanzibar, Dar-es-Salaam, Beira and then to Durban. We occasionally took one of two other British India liners, the *Kampala* or the *Karanja*, on business trips to the Seychelles. All of them were very elegant, very quiet passenger ships – the perfect 'tonic' in our long-distance travels. The British India liners were probably our very best favorites. They were very charming, friendly and cozy. It was an era of Goanese stewards in starched white jackets and ritual four o'clock teas, overhead fans and elephant tusks in the main lounge."

"We also travelled in the Italian-flag Lloyd Triestino liners – in ships like the *Africa* and *Europa*, the *Asia* and *Victoria*, and in the larger *Galileo Galilei* and *Guglielmo Marconi* after the closure of the Suez Canal meant that their Australian sailings had to be diverted via the Cape. They were always the most modern ships on the African runs, and were also the best appointed. Years ahead of the other companies at the time, their liners were completely air-conditioned. I can assure you that such an amenity was a great relief, especially when docked at places like Beira, with humid mid-afternoon temperatures as high as 112 degrees."

"Of course, there were incidents. We were aboard the Union-Castle *Bloemfontein Castle* when she made her heroic rescue of all hands from the wrecked Dutch liner *Klipfontein*, in January 1953. In those days, there was a terrific shortage of berths in South and East African ports. Often, freighters had to wait for three or four weeks. Liners had to wait for one week. At Beira, companies couldn't book a berth in advance. The first ship to arrive was given the berth. The *Klipfontein* hit a dangerous reef and was ripped open immediately. She sank in something like 45 minutes. But, due to the close proximity and alertness of the Union-Castle ship and her crew, everyone from the Dutch ship was saved. She had been evacuated in record time. However, everything else, including the valuable cargo, was lost."

"Also, on another occasion, when travelling between Walvis Bay and Cape Town in the *Durban Castle*, we recall the murder of Gay Gibson, an English passenger. It all made rather sensational headline news, especially since her body had been pushed through the porthole. I also recall the captain of another Union-Castle ship, during a trip in the Red Sea, when he was convinced he had seen a UFO. Supposedly he sighted it at three in the morning, but he was reluctant to send a message to the London head office. It seems he didn't want to disturb his chances of being appointed commodore."

"The Union-Castle ships, while always the largest and perhaps best-known passenger fleet trading to Africa, were never quite as good as the British India liners and certainly surpassed by the Lloyd Triestino fleet. However, when Union-Castle refitted [in the early 'sixties] the likes of the *Braemar Castle*, *Kenya Castle* and *Rhodesia Castle* – their 'Round Africa' ships – they were much better and made all-cabin class, which was actually equal to first class."

"Occasionally, when travelling to Britain, we would take an alternate, far longer route and cross the South Atlantic and travel via South America. Once, we took Royal Interocean Lines' *Tjitjalengka* from Durban to Rio.

From there, we were booked to London on Blue Star's *Brasil Star* when suddenly – and with just two hours notice! – we were given one of the best cabins on Moore-McCormack's *Argentina*, which was bound for Port Everglades. Once at Florida, we then decided to see something of the Bahamas and so booked a short weekend cruise on the Costa Line's *Franca C.* Upon return, we were then booked in P&O's *Oriana*, which was coming home from Australia to Southampton via the Panama and the Caribbean. Most unfortunately, she scraped a lock in the Panama Canal when one of her propellers snagged a lock gate. Twelve feet of the prop was wrecked and there was shaft damage as well. The *Oriana* was dragging badly. She had to proceed directly to Southampton and so the Port Everglades call was dropped. There was no other UK-bound ship for weeks. Instead, after checking that Bible-like reference piece, *The ABC Shipping Guide*, I discovered that the old *Queen Elizabeth* was due on her way from the Caribbean to New York. We then continued with her to Southampton."

Occasionally, Mr. and Mrs. Andresen would also travel in passenger-carrying cargo ships. Mrs. Andresen recalled, "Often, we enjoyed the very beautiful ships of the British-flag Ellerman Lines. I especially recall the 12-passenger *City of Hull*. It was sheer luxury. She had the most beautiful drawing room, the most splendid china, turbaned stewards and an Indian hairdresser who came to your cabin. Another delightful little vessel was the Dutch *Tjipanjet*, which carried 3 passengers. There was one double and one single. You could never buy a drink, however. Her jovial captain always insisted. Consequently, it was often said that he spent more money on his 3 passengers than did all of the combined captains of the far larger Royal Interocean liners *Ruys*, *Boissevain* and *Tegelberg*, which carried several hundred passengers each."

After the demise of the Union-Castle mail service to the Cape, a small combination vessel, the 3,100-ton *St Helena* run by Britain's Curnow Shipping started a new service, mainly to maintain the link with the remote island of St. Helena, but also to revive the liner service to South Africa. The Andresens included her in their travels. "Although she was such a small ship, she was remarkably comfortable. The entertainment was quite interesting considering that it was nothing more than records and tapes for dancing, staff-inspired games and some virtuosos among the crew. We travelled from Avonmouth to Cape Town via the Canaries and St. Helena and when one woman complained of the movement of the ship the captain promptly stood on his head to disprove such a protest. Among the cargo onboard our trip, I recall a young bull and 200 chickens."

Towards the end of 1983 the Andresens made another African passenger ship trip. They made the 'last voyage' in yet another combination liner, the 7,900-ton *Centaur*. Mr. Andresen recounted, "Formerly British and once used on the Singapore-Australia run, she was, by now Singapore-owned and had Singapore registry, but was chartered to Curnow Shipping. She had been used as a relief ship on the South Atlantic run to St. Helena and Cape Town, replacing the smaller *St Helena*, which was under charter to the British Government for extended duties in the Falklands."

"We booked a suite and spent six weeks onboard the *Centaur*, travelling from Avonmouth to Las Palmas, Ascension, St. Helena, Cape Town, Durban and then onwards to Mauritius, Fremantle and Singapore. Curnow operated her until Cape Town and then her Singapore owners, who still used the name Blue Funnel, resumed operations. At Durban, we took on a full load of South African families, who were migrating to Australia. At Fremantle, and as the South Africans left the ship, her funnel was repainted in Blue Funnel colors and she was prepared for one last short cruise to Singapore (an intended call at Christmas Island was cancelled at the very last minute), where she was to be laid-up (and later sold to the Chinese)."

"Actually, the *Centaur* – while delightful in almost all respects – was a very tender ship. It seems there was a misunderstanding during construction [at the John Brown shipyards at Clydebank, in 1963]. There was a serious miscalculation with her engine bed on the keel. Consequently, she was always very tender and when she was empty, she was very, very tender indeed. She always had several hundred tons of ballast and always carried reserves of food and water, which also served as a form of ballast. However, all of this reduced her cargo capacity and therefore made her less than an economical ship. It would have cost millions to put her right. During her very last days, as we sailed for Singapore, she began to suffer from engine trouble. Actually, her survey certificates had expired at Fremantle and her owners had to ask for a special one-week extension to continue the voyage. But, in all, she was a very fine ship for such a long voyage."

The great Union-Castle liners. In the 1950s, the *Pretoria Castle* was one of the Company's largest and fastest 'mailships', trading on the regular run between Southampton, Madeira or Las Palmas, Cape Town, Port Elizabeth, East London and Durban. At 28,705 tons, she could make 22 knots and carry 755 passengers (214 in first, 541 in tourist). She partook in the well-known tradition that every Thursday at 4 o'clock sharp, a Union-Castle liner carrying passengers and Her Majesty's Mails left Southampton Docks for the South African Cape. *Alex Duncan.*

The 17,000-ton *Rhodesia Castle* was used in the London-Round Africa service, a voyage that took nine weeks to complete. *Union-Castle Line.*

South of the Sahara:
The Farrell Lines

Farrell were for many years America's largest shipping line to Africa. They served three coasts, calling at most of the major ports 'south of the Sahara'. Farrell operations were divided into two sections and together these supported no less than 14 large freighters and 2 combination passenger-cargo liners (the 82-passenger *African Enterprise* and *African Endeavor*) in the mid 1950s.

The first service handled the West Coast of Africa, from Dakar south to Lobito, and included ports along the Gold Coast, the Ivory Coast, the Guinea Coast and the delta of the Congo River. American manufactured goods were delivered to these ports while the return manifests included local produce. The other, certainly more prestigious, perhaps more important service went to South and East Africa. Generally, it took 17 days at sea when sailing direct from New York (the Farrell Lines terminal was actually in Brooklyn) to Cape Town. The ships then continued onwards to Port Elizabeth, Durban, Lourenco Marques, Beira, Dar-es Salaam, Mombasa, Tanga and sometimes Zanzibar (especially to load cloves

and vanilla beans). Homeward to the US East Coast ports, Farrell ships delivered a vast array of goods: coffee, sisal, wattle bark, wool, hides, skins, chrome, copper, lobster tails, grapes, wines, spices, cashew nuts and on occasion a crate of ostrich feathers.

Having the strongest US trade link to South and East Africa, Farrell constantly had to keep pace. While the 7,900-ton *African Lightning* class of freighters were quite adequate for the 1950s, new ships were needed for the next decade. The Company added no less than five 14,000-tonners in the early '60s which were highly efficient, very fast and carried a dozen passengers in superb accommodations. This was the *African Neptune* class. Later, they moved into the containership business and also took over the Australian services of the American Pioneer Line, which had been a part of the United States Lines. But the continuously escalating costs of running American-flag ships coupled with fierce foreign competition led to some drastic changes by the 1990s. After buying out the remains of the American Export-Isbandtsen Lines, they have downsized to about a half-dozen containerships, and now trade to the Mediterranean and Middle East. After so many years, the African services ended for Farrell in 1979.

The 1946-built *African Rainbow* sails from Cape Town, continuing her voyage along the South and East African coasts. She was one of six sisterships in the Farrell fleet and had a gross tonnage of 7,900 and a service speed of 16½ knots. Like many freighters she had accommodations for 12 passengers and fares for the 20-day voyage from New York to the Cape were priced from $550 in the early 1950s. She had 25 years of service with Farrell and then, after a further two years in lay-up, she was broken up on Taiwan in 1973.
Fred Rodriguez Collection.

One of Farrell's last traditional breakbulk freighters, the 1961-built *African Comet*, proudly wears the Company crest on her bow as she loads cargo at Brooklyn.

On another occasion, during a seamen's strike, three Farrell freighters have missed their African sailings and remain nested together. They are the sisterships *African Dawn*, *African Neptune* and *African Meteor*.
both photographs: Fred Rodriguez Collection.

Portugal's colonial interests in Africa supported a good number of passenger ships in the 1950s and '60s. Although seen here passing through the Kiel Canal in 1952 during a cruise to the Baltic, the 8,200-ton *Serpa Pinto* was one of the oldest Portugese passenger ships in African service during the 1950s. She had originally been *Ebro* of the Royal Mail Lines, built in 1915.

More modern was the Companhia Colonial's 21,700-ton *Vera Cruz*. Originally intended for the Lisbon-Rio de Janeiro trade, she later spent much of her time carrying troops as well as passengers to Luanda, Lobito, Mocamedes, Cape Town, Lourenco Marques, Beira and Nacala. Behind her is her twin sister, the *Santa Maria* which sailed to the Caribbean and Florida. *both photographs: Luis Miguel Correia Collection.*

Completed in 1951 and shown anchored in the River Mersey, the 14,000-ton *Aureol* was the pride of Britain's Elder Dempster Lines. She traded for over twenty years to such West African ports as Takoradi, Freetown and Lagos.
Alex Duncan.

Her fleetmates included the smaller sisterships *Accra* (also shown in the Mersey) and *Apapa*, both of which were supported by a brisk British colonial trade until the 1960s.
Frank O. Braynard Collection.

Regular visitors to the South African Cape in the 1950s included the Lloyd Triestino *Africa* (above), which came from Genoa via the Suez Canal; Holland-Africa Line's *Jagersfontein* (centre), which traded from Amsterdam and Southampton; and another Dutchman, the *Ruys* (bottom) of Royal Interocean Lines, which sailed on a very extensive itinerary from the East Coast of South America to South and East Africa, Southeast Asia and then along the Far East as far as Japan.

Photos Roger Sherlock, Holland-Africa Line & Royal Interocean Lines.

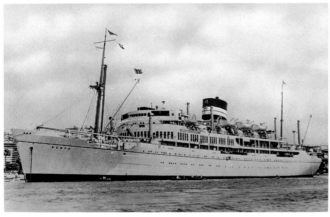

Built in 1948, the 10,300-ton passenger-cargo liner *Karanja* of the British India Steam Navigation Company, Limited sailed regularly between East Africa and India. Beginning at Durban, she would call at Lourenco Marques, Beira, Dar-es-Salaam, Zanzibar, Mombasa, the Seychelles and then at Karachi, Bedibunder, Porebunder and finally Bombay. The 16-knot ship could carry some 1,050 passengers – 60 in first class, 180 in second class and over 800 in third class. Noted for their excellent cuisine and fine service, she and her sister, the *Kampala*, were very popular ships for well over two decades. Shown loading at Kilindini in Kenya, the *Karanja* also had 5 cargo holds. *P&O Group.*

The largest passenger ships in the British India fleet were the near-sisters *Kenya* (pictured) and *Uganda*. Built in 1951-52, they had large cargo capacities blended with accommodations for some 300 passengers, approximately 200 in very comfortable first class and 100 in tourist class. Providing a well-travelled link between Britain and her East African colonies, these ships were routed from London via Gibraltar, Malta, Port Said and Aden, and then onwards to Mombasa, Tanga, Zanzibar, Dar-es-Salaam and Beira. *P&O Group.*

Spain's Naviera Aznar ran a service to the Canary Islands from both London and Liverpool. Their combo ships, which returned to Britain with large amounts of bananas, tomatos and other fruits, also carried passengers. Shown at Liverpool, the 4,600-ton *Monte Arucas* had very comfortable accommodations for 36 passengers. *Roger Sherlock.*

Because of their obvious colonial connection to Algeria and Tunisia, the French ran a good number of passenger and passenger-cargo ships across the western Mediterranean out of Marseilles. The 4,500-ton *Gouverneur Général Chanzy* was amongst the eldest by the late 1950s. She dated from 1922. *Eric W. Johnson Collection.*

The 10,100-ton *Ville D'Alger*, built in 1935, was one of the fastest, having a service speed of over 21 knots. She ran regular voyages to Oran, Algiers, Philippeville and Tunis. During the War she was set afire and sunk but was salvaged and restored. Now she had one funnel instead of her original two. *Eric W. Johnson Collection.*

American-built locomotives are being offloaded by a floating heavy-lift crane at Durban. They are coming off Moore-McCormack Lines' *Mormacpenn*. Holland-America's *Axeldyk* is in the background.
Peter Lancaric Collection.

A twin-funnel South African Railways tug assists the US-flag *Robin Kettering* of the Robin Line, as she departs from Durban. Busily, berths were almost immediately reoccupied.
Frank O. Braynard Collection.

Freight being handled aboard a Robin Line freighter, the *Robin Hood*, at Durban with two British India Line ships in the background. *Peter Lancaric Collection.*

Ellerman Lines were well-known not only for their luxurious combo liners, but also for their 12-passenger freighters. (top) In this panoramic view from the 1950s, three Company ships are in the Cape Town docks (from left to right) the *City of Pretoria*, the *City of Brooklyn* and the *City of Lille*. In the second view, two muscular tugs are assisting the 8,450-ton *City of Pretoria* in the Turning Basin at East London. The South Africans used coal-fired steam tugs far longer than most because, while they had plenty of coal, international embargos made it difficult for them to import oil. *Cunard-Ellerman Group.*

Chapter Four
East of Suez

P&O-Orient Memories

"In 1954, there was a great void in Pacific Ocean travel," remembers Dean Miller, who has been the public relations officer at Vancouver for the P&O-Orient Lines and its successor, Princess Cruises, for nearly 40 years. "The big pre-World War Two Canadian Pacific liner service to the Far East was never restored and the Union Line's old *Aorangi*, which ran from Australia and New Zealand up to Vancouver, had just been retired. And so, the British-flag Orient Line, which normally ran its liners out from London to Australian ports via the Suez Canal, decided to experiment with an extended service. Ships would go up from Sydney to Vancouver via Auckland, Suva and Honolulu, and then return via San Francisco and Los Angeles. The first sailing was made by the 27,000-ton *Oronsay*, one of the Orient Line's newest liners and then two other trips by the old, 1935-built *Orion*. The first responses were encouraging, especially because of wartime marriages. Many American GIs had gone to Australia and married local girls; from Australia and New Zealand servicemen had come up to Canada for training and had married Canadian girls. By the 1950s, there were children and even grandchildren involved. This was Orient Line's success at first and meant 12 voyages within three years, by 1957."

The Orient Line's success led to discussions with their parent company, P&O (The Peninsular & Oriental Steam Navigation Co. Ltd.). 'Let's make the Pacific a British Ocean' became their theme. And so, the Orient Line's *Orcades*, *Oronsay* and *Orsova* were joined by P&O's *Himalaya*, *Chusan*, *Arcadia* and *Iberia*. P&Os appearance meant also expansion to the Far East. Their *Chusan*, in regular London-Far East service, subsequently made the first Far East-Vancouver passage. By early 1958, it all had fallen into place with the *Himalaya's* inaugural trip from Auckland and Wellington to Vancouver.

While P&O was larger and better known, the Orient Line was also distinguished in its own right. At first the partnership was known as Orient & Pacific Lines, but soon gave way to P&O Orient Lines. Differences between ships remained, however. According to Dean Miller, "P&O had staff captains on its liners whereas Orient Line had staff commanders. The Orient liners perhaps had slightly more prestige and were more comparable to the famous Atlantic liners of those years. For example, the *Orcades*, the *Oronsay* and the *Orsova* each had a first class grill room that was placed aft and looked over the stern section through floor-to-ceiling windows. There was an added fee for admittance even for first class passengers. Expectedly, there was more variety in the Grill Room menus, perhaps better service than first class and certainly more caviar and special desserts."

"Inevitably, the P&O-Orient liners were thought to be 'luxury liners' because of their size at almost 30,000 tons and carrying nearly 1,500 passengers in two classes," added Dean Miller. "But really they were 'passenger ships'. They were nice, comfortable, multi-purpose ships. Their first class was very pleasant with burl woodwork, oversized chairs and a spacious feel. But it was not luxurious. Tourist class, however, had far smaller cabins, all upper and lower bunks, and unconcealed pipes along the cabin ceilings. But the fares in those days, even by the early 1960s, were a big contribution to their success. They began at $17 a day – a fantastic bargain! You almost couldn't afford to stay at home."

Two rather spectacular liners, in fact the biggest away from the Atlantic run, were added in 1961-62. The 44,000-ton *Canberra* and the 41,000-ton *Oriana* would be the last of this P&O-Orient Lines service. They were hugely successful for some years but the jets eventually stole away their trade. By the mid-1970s, they were sailing for P&O Cruises instead.

Today, Dean Miller welcomes a new generation of passenger ships to Vancouver. The likes of the two-class, 27,000-ton *Himalaya* and *Orcades* have given way to the *Crown Princess* and the *Regal Princess*, 70,000-ton megacruiseships. "It has all changed so much," lamented Miller as he peered over the waters of Vancouver harbor from his downtown offices.

(opposite top) **P&O's magnificent 44,000-ton *Canberra*, completed in 1961 and for a time the largest liner ever built for a service other than the North Atlantic, passes before San Francisco's Ferry Building as she heads for Southampton via the Panama Canal and the Caribbean. On an around-the-World voyage of some 100 days, she had arrived from Australia, New Zealand and Hawaii, and had stopped at Vancouver.** *P&O Group.*

(opposite) **Very few companies can equal the historic position of Britain's P&O Lines, The Peninsular & Oriental Steam Navigation Company. During the peak of the British Empire, P&O served as the major link to her many possessions east of Suez. For more than a century, the lounges and decks and cabins of P&O ships were filled by British colonials – the military men, the administrators, managers, merchants and traders all travelled 'out East' on 'the P&O'. Even the Viceroy of India himself used P&O passenger ships. They sailed from London to India, Malaya, the China stations and Australia. This atmospheric view from the foredeck of the liner *Strathnaver* shows the expanse of the Suez Canal.** *P&O Group.*

The classic lines of the 1932-built *Strathnaver* are shown in this view as she departs from Sydney for the five-week voyage to London via Melbourne, Adelaide, Fremantle, Colombo, Bombay, Aden and Gibraltar.
P&O Group.

In another view, dating from November 1966, the liner *Oronsay* passes under the Sydney Harbor Bridge. Long associated with the larger P&O Company, the 'O Boats' of the Orient Line were finally merged as P&O-Orient in 1960, but then the singular P&O name was readopted six years later.
P&O Group.

In the late 1950s, the P&O and Orient liners began to sail more heavily in Pacific waters, which included voyages up to the North American West Coast. Soon, the schedules of these companies would include voyages of up to four months that might touch on over 100 different ports. In this scene, at Suva on Fiji, two P&O-Orient liners meet: the *Arcadia* is already docked while the *Oronsay* is just arriving. *P&O Group.*

Philip Jackson was attracted to the great P&O company soon after the Second World War, in January 1946. "They had an appealing blend of both liners and freighters," he recalled, "and they sailed to exotic places – like India and the Far East. Actually, it was most unusual for me to apply to P&O, having come from the *Conway*, an old sailing vessel used as a training ship while berthed in the Menai Straits on the north coast of Wales. The Blue Funnel Line was the primary sponsor of the *Conway* and most of her 250 cadets joined that Liverpool firm. P&O was linked to another merchant training ship, the *Worcester*, which was moored in the Thames."

After joining P&O, Jackson went from cadet to cadet officer within twelve months. He had his second mate's ticket at twenty. His first ship was the 7,700-ton *Socotra* (pictured here). "We sailed from London's Royal Docks and then several North European ports [Bremen, Antwerp and Rotterdam] on four-month roundtrips

to Australia and back. Outwards, we carried mostly general cargo: manufactured goods, motor cars, steel and cement. Homewards, we had sheepskins, wool, timber and tinned fruit."

Afterward, Jackson joined several other P&O cargo liners, among them the 524-foot long *Somali*. "She worked the Far East run – to Malaysia, Hong Kong, China, Japan and the Philippines. Onboard, we brought home timber, tinned fish, egg pulp (from China to East Germany, but offloaded at Hamburg and then reshipped), rubber, latex, palm oil and the beginning of the inexpensive products, such as toys and other plastic items, that are now so much associated with the East." *P&O Group.*

Busy Yokohama: The P&O flagship *Canberra* was the largest passenger liner ever to visit Japan when she called at Yokohama's South Pier on March 15th 1966. The 44,700-ton liner received a gala fireboat reception and was berthed just aft of another P&O ship, the combo liner *Chitral*, and just across from the *George Anson* and the world cruiseship *Sagafjord*. The latter ship, owned by the Norwegian America Line and completed in the Fall of 1965, was also on her maiden visit to Japanese ports. *P&O Group.*

For some thirty or so years following the Second World War, there was massive migration to Australia and New Zealand. Dozens of passenger ships, many of them converted and quite austere, were used to carry low-fare passengers from such far-off ports as London, Southampton, Bremerhaven, Rotterdam, Genoa, Naples and Piraeus. With passenger fares often underwritten by the Australian Government,

which wanted to build a vast labor source, the cost might be as little as £10 for these four-to-six week 'assisted passages'. Built in 1925 for the Donaldson Line's Glasgow-Montreal service as the *Letitia*, this 14,000-tonner was sold to the British government in 1946 to become the peacetime troopship *Empire Brent* and later the migrant ship *Captain Cook*. Shown passing through the Panama Canal on a voyage from the UK to New Zealand, she carried 1,088 all-third class passengers. Her return sailings were used by budget tourists and some reverse migrants who could not adjust to life 'Down Under'.
James L. Shaw Collection.

One of the finest and fastest liners on the Australia-New Zealand run from the UK was Shaw, Savill & Albion's 26,400-ton *Dominion Monarch*. Built in 1939, she was, in fact, a passenger ship with a very large cargo capacity. In her six holds, there was space for 650,000 cubic feet of cargo. The majority was refrigerated, particularly for the meat brought home to Britain. Her passenger quarters were of the highest standard and might best be described as 'club-like'. She carried only 508 passengers, all of them in first class. She is, however, shown in 1961, departing from Glasgow Wharf at Wellington on her final return sailing to London. After a short stint as a floating hotel at Seattle for the 1962 World's Fair, she sailed to Japan (as the *Dominion Monarch Maru*) and the breaker's yard. *Vincent Messina Collection.*

Britain's Anchor Line maintained a passenger-cargo service between Liverpool, Karachi and Bombay. Among their ships was the 1948-built motor ship *Caledonia*, which carried 304 one-class passengers in extremely comfortable accommodation. *Alex Duncan.*

For over a century, the British India Steam Navigation Company operated services between various segments of the British Empire and later the British Commonwealth. The *Santhia*, shown at her Hong Kong moorings, sailed between India, Malaya, Hong Kong and Japan. Note the large number of lifeboats. On some sections of their routes British India ships carried huge numbers of deck passengers. *Alex Duncan.*

British India also maintained a large cargo ship fleet. The 1951-built *Chakdina* was one of 13 'C Class' freighters and she sailed in the Company's India-Australia service. *Frank O. Braynard Collection.*

British India's famous old *Rajula*, normally in service between India and Malaysia, is shown on a special visit to Hong Kong's Kowloon Bay in September 1957. She was bound for a dockyard and an extensive overhaul. Built at Glasgow in 1926, she had, for a time after her delivery, one of the greatest peacetime passenger-certificates – for over 5,000 people, many of whom were deck passengers. An 8,500-tonner, she had triple-expansion steam engines which gave her a service speed of just 12 knots. When she was finally retired in 1973 at the age of forty-eight, she was still so well liked that loyalists wanted to preserve her as a museum, a floating reminder of the great colonial passenger ships. Instead, however, she sailed for two more years as the Indian-flag *Rangat* before being scrapped at Bombay. *P&O Group.*

Long-haul services from Europe to the East included ships such as the French combo-liner *Cambodge*, belonging to Messageries Maritimes. At 13,200 tons, she carried up to 347 passengers in three classes along with considerable freight. A fast ship capable of 21 knots, she traded between Marseilles, Port Said, Suez, Aden, Djibouti, Bombay, Colombo, Singapore, Saigon, Manila, Hong Kong, Kobe and Yokohama. *Eric Johnson Collection.*

Until the 1960s, combination passenger-cargo liners were both very common and very popular in Eastern services. Bibby Line's 8,900-ton *Leicestershire* carried up to 75 passengers on the run between Liverpool and Rangoon. *Bibby Line.*

Another British shipowner, the Glen Line, used such ships as the 18-passenger *Denbighshire* on their service to the Far East. She is shown alongside a Japanese freighter at Genoa in June 1963. *Michael Cassar.*

P&O's *Chitral*, shown at Valletta on Malta, also ran to the Orient. A 14,000-tonner, formerly a Belgian colonial liner, she carried some 200 passengers in very comfortable, all-first class quarters. *P&O Group.*

Shaw Savill's *Gothic*, built in 1948 and used in 1953-54 for the Royal Tour of Queen Elizabeth II, normally carried up to 85 all-first class passengers on the run from London to Auckland and Wellington via Panama.
V.H. Young and Len Sawyer Collection.

The Dutch Blue Funnel

The Blue Funnel Line, based in Liverpool, had a huge fleet in the 1950s, some of the ships known as the 'Blue Flues'. They had a number of subsidiaries as well. They even had a Dutch-flag arm, which operated as the NSMO also known as the Associated Dutch Company.

"By the mid 1970's, there were 6 cargo ships owned by Blue Funnel that were still under the Dutch flag. These were the last," according to Dutch-born Captain Hans Mateboer, who is today master of Holland America Line cruiseships. "These ships were each owned separately by a member of the Blue Funnel Group such as the Elder Dempster Lines, the Glen Line and the Henderson Line. This Dutch-flag arm dated back one hundred years, to the 1870s, when Blue Funnel wanted to gain entry into the trade to the Dutch East Indies, now Indonesia. It was much easier using a Dutch flag. It lasted for decades and did not begin to decline until the 1950s, but then there was also an interesting reversal. Because of obvious political reasons, the British-flag ships had open entry into Indonesian ports but the Dutch ships were more welcome in Malaysia. Both countries were having difficult 'post-colonial periods.'

Captain Mateboer served aboard two of the older Blue Funnel freighters, the *Machaon* and the *Eumaeus*, both typically named from the Greek Iliad. "It was a great learning experience aboard these ships for a young seafarer such as myself," the Captain recalled. "The radar was usually inoperative so we relied on our own navigational skills. And no Blue Funnel ship was insured because they had such high standards. It was also Company policy to follow fixed routes at all times. For example, we always sailed on a direct course from Gibraltar to Malta and then from Malta to Port Said. This meant we could always help one another. There was always another Blue Funnel ship not more than 2-3 days away that could offer assistance. And on these older ships, you could dismantle parts of the bridge for better ventilation, especially in the notorious Red Sea. And onboard the *Eumaeus* [7,841 tons, built 1953], there was still a gun cabinet in my cabin."

These ships were routed from North European ports (Hamburg, Rotterdam, Antwerp and various UK ports) to the Iberian peninsular (Oporto or Vigo) and then through the Suez to Indonesia, to Djakarta and at least a dozen smaller ports. "We carried a variety of European manufactured goods out and then loaded what is considered the best tobacco in the world at Sumatra," added Captain Mateboer. "We then went up to Japan, to Kobe, Yokohama and Nagasaki, to load 'CKD' cargo, 'completely knocked down' auto parts – the doors, fenders, even engines. At Hong Kong, Bangkok and Singapore, we'd load mostly electronics. And finally, but only if there was space, we'd take on tea at Colombo in Ceylon."

In the age of rapid and efficient containerization and other shifts in worldwide cargo shipping, this Dutch-flag service ended in 1978. Today, Blue Funnel is barely involved in shipping. "There was a special romance to shipping even in the 1970s. Today, it has all changed so much," concluded Hans Mateboer.

Blue Funnel Line's *Helenus* worked the UK-Australia trade. She had accommodations for up to 30 passengers and she would return home to Liverpool well loaded with wool, flax, wheat and such refrigerated items as mutton, fruits, butter, cheese, eggs and rabbits. Legend has it that when Alfred Holt founded Blue Funnel back in 1853 the stores on his first ship included a quantity of light blue paint, which, in thrifty fashion, the crew applied to the stack and thereby established a tradition. In 1960, Blue Funnel had a fleet of over 60 ships, all of them recognizable by their distinctive profile and funnel colors and their often hard-to-pronounce names from Greek mythology. *Alex Duncan.*

Dutch Sisters in the Orient

Holland's Royal Interocean Lines ran one of the largest passenger ship networks of all time. Their longest route, which employed no less than 5 passenger ships, stretched from the East Coast of South America over to the South African Cape, then to Malaysia and Singapore and finally all the way along the Far East to Japan. This meant that passengers could sail from Rio de Janeiro aboard a ship like the 14,000-ton *Ruys* and be in Yokohama three months later. Then there were other services as well such as India to Australia and one from Australia to the Far East. In the 1950s and 1960s, Royal Interocean had over 50 ships in service. Although Dutch, their main office was in Singapore.

The *Tjiluwah*. *C.B. Mulholland*.

Dr David Kirkman, a ship's doctor on Australian and Far Eastern passenger ships of all flags for many years, fondly remembered Royal Interocean and their ships. "Royal Interocean Lines passenger service was often abbreviated to RIL, which was known as Relax-In-Luxury. Their larger ships, like the *Ruys*, ran a three-class service. They carried all types of passengers – from old Dutch colonials to rich Chinese merchants, to Malaysian and Indian migrant workers. Onboard, they had the expected Dutch tropical ambiance: lots of rattan furniture, overhead fans, plenty of dark wood panelling."

But two of Dr Kirkman's favorite ships were smaller ones, the 8,600-ton sisterships *Tjiwangi* and *Tjiluwah* (pictured above). Built in Holland in 1951, they had Indonesian names and accommodations for as few as 98 passengers in first class and only 120 in second class. There was also originally space for some deck passengers as well. "Unfortunately, these ships were designed just a bit too late for the Dutch colonial inter-island service in the East Indies for which they were intended," noted Dr Kirkman. "So instead, Royal Interocean created a new Asean service just for them – from Melbourne, Sydney and Brisbane. Then they'd sail on an 11-day non-stop voyage to Yokkaichi (a Japanese port in Ise Bay, near Nagoya) to offload our most precious cargo: Australian wool. From there, we'd go to Nagoya, then Yokohama and finally Kobe. Then over to Keelung and to Kaohsiung on Taiwan. Afterwards, we'd have a 4-day layover in Hong Kong before sailing directly back to Brisbane. Homewards, we carried much lighter cargoes: tinned fruit, textiles, clothing and those small, inexpensive manufactured goods from Taiwan. But there was such a contrast in labor amongst these ports. The Australian dockers at Melbourne took a week to load the same cargo that the Japanese handled in a single day!"

"Beautifully decorated and superbly maintained," according to Dr Kirkman, "these two ships were known to Australians as the 'big white yachts'. They had a two-month roundtrip that was very popular with wealthier, retired Australians."

In the early 1970s, when both the *Tjiwangi* and the *Tjiluwah* turned twenty, they required huge, expensive refits to meet new maritime codes. This seemed uneconomic to Royal Interocean. Consequently, the pair was sold to Singapore buyers, the Pacific International Lines, and renamed *Kota Bali* and *Kota Singapura* respectively. They were put on the shorter Singapore-Fremantle run, but purely as passenger-cruise ships. Cargo was no longer carried. They were quite successful for a time, offering cruises to Australian travellers mostly. "But they were very much downgraded," added Dr Kirkman. "They were clearly aimed at the budget market. They were poorly maintained. I was very saddened to visit them in later years and notice the dirty conditions, the cigarette burns and the greasy grime that prevailed even in the passenger areas."

Ironically, the aged *Kota Bali* finished her days in that old Indonesian inter-island trade. She travelled between Surabaya and Makassar, ferrying passengers as well as having secondhand cars stowed on her decks. Reportedly, her general condition grew worse still. Today, while both ships have long since been scrapped, they provide us with an interesting glimpse into some long-ago passenger ship services – 'On the wool run to Yokkaichi…!'

With the Norwegians to the Far East

Marketed in North America as the Barber Lines (named for their agents, the Barber Steamship Company), the Norwegian shipowner Wilh. Wilhelmsen – the Wilhelmsen Lines to some – had one of the World's largest freighter fleets in the 1950s and '60s. Their black-hulled ships with their numerous masts, kingposts and booms, and their 'T names', were especially familiar on the routes out to the Far East. They sailed from Europe as well as North American ports. And until the age of full containerships in the 1970s, they were known for their passenger services. Their ships carried from 4 to 12 passengers and were special favorites with 'freighter travel enthusiasts'.

"I sailed with Wilhelmsen about a half-dozen times,

mostly from Europe, but also from New York and New Orleans," recalled Jan Solheim. "I enjoyed the tranquillity, the utter relaxation and peace that their long voyages offered. I especially remember the *Tomar*. About 6,000 tons and built just after the War, in 1948, she could carry up to 10 passengers. Housed just on two decks, the Lower Bridge Deck and the Main Deck, she had two doubles with private bathrooms, four singles with communicating bathrooms between each and a very spacious owner's suite for two. They were the sort of rooms in which passengers could make themselves feel very much at home, which was a good point considering the long time you were likely to be onboard the ship. The large lounge was very charming, with soft chairs and sofas. The dining room was typically Scandinavian, very home-like and served the highest standard of Norwegian fare. It might be interesting to note that these Wilhelmsen freighters had stewardesses in the dining room rather than stewards. The Norwegian officers were usually very congenial and most accommodating. You were treated almost as an equal to the cargo below, which onboard a freighter is quite a consideration. The officers joined us for meals and occasionally on the open decks, where a canvas pool was sometimes erected."

"The voyages were often very long and could last as much as a month more than intended. Once, onboard the *Tomar*, we sailed for just one day short of 5 months. We started at Oslo and then called at Hamburg, Rotterdam, Antwerp, Lisbon and Marseilles before passing through the Suez Canal and then headed for Port Sudan, Aden, Singapore, Hong Kong, Manila, some very small backwater ports in the Philippines, Kobe and finally the turnaround at Yokohama. We called at almost the same ports on the return to Oslo. The round trip fare in 1954 was a little less than £400."

"The passengers were a very curious, but always interesting lot," added Mr. Solheim. "There were retired people, families being reassigned and, in the summer months, the school teachers. I also remember an Italian count, a British admiral from World War One and an Indian prince, who claimed to be travelling with £1 million in jewels that he hoped to sell in London. Then there were the two American ladies who were regulars and who made round trips from New York just to buy large amounts of furniture in Hong Kong

and the Philippines. It would travel home with them in the holds below. There was lots of machinery and manufactured goods going out to the East in those days. But we returned with more interesting items – Chinese silks, plastic toys from Japan, electronics from Hong Kong, spices and teas and tobaccos. And there was liquid latex. It was very interesting. Going with the Norwegians had great romance about it."

Two Wilhelmsen freighters: the *Texas* (opposite page) in wintertime Baltic waters and the *Teneriffa* (above) at Mobile, Alabama. *Frank O. Braynard Collection.*

Sailing with Ellermans

When Ian Taylor joined what was then one of the World's mightiest shipping companies, Britain's Ellerman Lines, in those last dark days of the Second World War, in 1944, he felt he could see the future of the shipping business with great certainty. But contrarily, he could never have imagined what the next decades would bring: the collapse of the traditional breakbulk freighter, the dissolution of well-established passenger trades and finally, and possibly worst of all, the virtual disappearance of historic shipowners like Ellermans. And at the same time, he would witness the rise of mammoth containerships and new, often Third World shipowners.

When I met Captain Taylor in London in 1990, he had clear, succinct memories of his Ellerman years, the Company ships, their trades and the cargoes carried. And he regretted that the passing had come all too quickly and dramatically.

The young Taylor went across to Baltimore in November 1944 to join a brand new Liberty ship, the 7,200-ton, 11-knot *Samois*, which was being loaned out to the M.O.W.T., the British Ministry of War Transport, but with Ellermans as managers. "Our first cargo was army goods going out to the troops at Calcutta," he recalled. "We finally got away on April 30th 1945, the same day that President Franklin D. Roosevelt died. It was very, very sad. I remember hearing on the radio Bing Crosby singing FDR's favorite's song 'Don't Fence Me In'. We sailed with our flags at half mast."

When the War ended, Taylor was

Among the many ships used by Ellerman in their Australian service were the 7,700-ton *City of Wellington* (above), a 507-foot long ship built in 1956, and the *City of London* (opposite page), an 8,400-ton ship completed in 1947. *both photographs: Cunard-Ellerman Group.*

assigned to many of the diverse Ellerman services, some of which were run with a New York-based shipping agent, Norton, Lilly & Company. (Many Americans believed that Norton, Lilly actually owned the ships, even with their British registry.) Special trade names had been created for the different routes such as the American & African Line, the American & Indian Line and the American & Australian Line. The voyages of the ships were actually divided – Ellermans would look after some portions while those New York-based affiliates were responsible for others. For example, one of Taylor's early ships, the solid-looking, 8,100-ton *City of Pretoria*, built just before the War started, in 1938, sailed under Ellerman while in ballast from Britain to New York. "Once there, however, she loaded for South and East African ports, but under the American & African Line," recalled Captain Taylor. "She

took on cargo not only at New York, but at Boston, Baltimore and Hampton Roads before crossing the South Atlantic to Cape Town, Port Elizabeth, East London, Durban, Lourenco Marques and finally to Beira. We were usually full-up in those years, the late 1940s, with American manufactured goods. But as we offloaded those US goods, we took on other items – fruits, tobacco and copper – for the voyage back up to British and North European ports that reverted to Ellerman direct control. And so, the ships in those years rotated and filled slots and came under various operators."

Later he was posted to the *City of Carlisle* which primarily sailed in the American & Australian Line service. She brought general cargo from the US East Coast ports to Australia and New Zealand, then changed back to Ellerman and brought a different cargo up to the UK.

From there, to restart the process, she went in ballast across to New York and so completed a world voyage. "On those outward voyages in the late '40s, we had more than enough of the American manufactured goods, but also some speciality items like paper from Newfoundland," added Taylor. "Going back to the UK, usually via Suez, we carried wool, tons and tons of it! We also had fruits and wines and meats, of course, in the freezer hold. Sometimes we had other chilled goods as well, like eggs."

After leaving the American East Coast, ships like the upright, 1945-built *City of Carlisle* stopped at Curacao for fuel before passing through the Panama Canal and into the Pacific. "It took 4 weeks to reach New Zealand and Australia at 16 knots," added the Captain. "After Sydney, Melbourne, Fremantle and others, we'd sail for Europe. Our first Continental port was either Dunkirk or Antwerp and then over to either London and Hull or Avonmouth and Liverpool. In all, it took 5 months for a full voyage, UK to UK."

"Time in port was quite different then," added the Captain. "It was quite unlike the very fast turnarounds for today's cost-conscious containerships. Then, we'd have a week's stay in New York, at the old Bush Terminal docks in Brooklyn. We could go ashore. I remember that a ticket for the Metropolitan Opera cost $2 and that was sitting in the aisle! The English pound had just been devalued from about $4 to about $2.80, and so many of the crew took time to give a pint of blood for which they received $5. That was 'big bucks' in those days!"

"But when you worked, you worked hard and long," he added. "I remember working all night on the *City of Dieppe*. She had 'specials' – cargo that needed special stowage, perhaps because it was small or fragile or perhaps very valuable. The Company Officer had to check these all the time. It was essential to have great rapport with the docking foremen. Sometimes, we would not finish until 6 the next morning."

Captain Taylor also served with another Ellerman-affiliate, the American & Indian Line. He sailed that service in the 12-passenger *City of Coventry*. "We'd do the usual US East Coast ports beginning or ending at New York and then sail direct to Port Said and the Suez Canal," he noted.

"Next, we'd stop at Aden for fuel and then sail for Karachi. Altogether it usually took 22-23 days. After Karachi, the *City of Coventry* would make a circuit of Indian, Sri Lankan and Pakistani ports and would occasionally head for Mombasa in East Africa, then finally homewards to New York via the Suez and the Med. The Indian ports in those days had great losses in mechanization. Their dockside cranes, for example, even had less load factors than the ship's cranes. But it was made up in manpower – the pure, brute strength of the Indian dockers."

"We also carried a dozen or so passengers on these Ellerman freighters," he added. "They were usually full-up every trip. We'd have business people and their families, Company managers, missionaries, but mostly elderly ladies making the roundtrip of some 75 or as much as 100-days or even more."

"Then there was some pretty nasty weather, especially on the Indian run," he added. "The Monsoon Season, which is actually heavy cyclonic weather, came in mid-June. It 'knocked us out' for at least 3 days in port. You would be gasping in the heat and then the heavy rains would cool you down, – well at least your temperature would drop. Your clothes remained damp. There had been dust everywhere and then, after the rain, mud everywhere. Dockside transport was halted completely!"

Captain Taylor spent a couple of years in the mid '50s aboard one of Ellerman's finest ships, the combination passenger-cargo liner *City of Exeter*. At 13,300 tons, she and her three sisters (*City of Durban, City of Port Elizabeth* and *City of York*) each had especially fine, all-first class quarters for 107 passengers. They sailed in regular frequency between London, Newcastle or Middlesbrough, Hamburg, Rotterdam, Antwerp and then back to London before heading south via Las Palmas in the Canaries to Cape Town, Port Elizabeth, East London, Durban, Lourenco Marques and finally a turnaround at Beira. It was 16 days from London to Cape Town and the full London-to-London roundtrip in seven weeks. The Company also offered 'mini cruises' from London up to Newcastle or Middlesbrough and then over to Hamburg, Rotterdam and Antwerp, and then back to London. These took about a week.

"The *City of Exeter* also carried about 10,000 tons of cargo, but as a passenger ship, she was like a big yacht," remembered the Captain. "The service ratio, for example, was extraordinary. Everything about her – the décor, the cuisine, the service – was magnificent. She had 69 Calcutta stewards, but needed an additional 8 European staff as well. We catered mostly to English passengers, usually 50 and older. Many were going on South African holidays – winter stays, family visits, safaris, garden tours. But some preferred making the full roundtrip as a sort of cruise-holiday."

In 1971, the 541-foot long *City of Exeter* and her sisters were retired and sold off. They had about fifteen years of good, profitable service, but by the early '70s, the jets had begun to lure away their passengers and that first generation of containerships their cargoes. "It was traumatic to see those beautiful combo liners go," added the Captain.

"It was the end of an era, the end for all those traditional passenger ships services that we knew so well and that had been around for decades, centuries even. Now, the airlines ruled. And even if the *City of Exeter* and her sisters still had some loyal and regular passengers, they needed huge and expensive surveys and upgrading. This, of course, was the final blow. It sealed their fates. The era of the passenger vessel as I knew it was over."

Company freighters began their decline even earlier, actually starting in the late 1950s. "The decline of companies like Ellermans was gradual. It started with so-called 'third party' competitors," added Captain Taylor. "Suddenly, there were lots of extra companies, smaller ones and many from the United States, but often with Greek shipowners in the background. Lucrative American Government aid items had gone out in Ellerman ships, but now were going in these other ships. In fact, when Ellerman began to sell-off some of their own ships, they often reappeared, renamed and repainted and therefore disguised somewhat, but as rivals to the very Company that had created them in the first place!"

One by one, the likes of the affiliate American & African Line and the American & Indian Line closed down completely. They could not compete. "We had to sell more and more freighters by the mid '60s. The older, 12-passenger types went first," added the Captain. "There were big changes and then that big British Seamen's Strike in '66. It was felt that there was a big gap between Ellerman management and the seagoing staff. We actually kept going a little longer, but only because of having Indian crews on our ships. They didn't want to get involved. These Indian crews had strong traditions, often long associations with the likes of the Ellerman Lines. It had been father to son to his son!"

The complete end came by the late '60s. "It was contraction all the way," he said. "Breakbulk freighters were just about finished, clearly redundant. From '68 onwards, it was containerization. One ACT containership, for example, suddenly took the place of 7 or 8 ordinary freighters. Ellerman co-operated with the Ben Line to cut costs and become more competitive and then, in 1973, merged everything as Ellerman City Lines. Costs were cut even further and manning levels lowered. The competition was fierce, the mood almost ferocious, the future uncertain."

By the late '70s, Captain Taylor was one of two Fleet Directors for Ellerman. "We still had 40 ships in the fleet, 20 for each of us to look after," he noted. "But by the early 1980s, we were down to 20 altogether. Later, there was more reorganization, more trimming, more cuts. We had 6 ships by the late '80s."

Taylor finally retired in 1988, just short of 45 years with what had become a greatly demoded British shipping company. "It was a different world by then – different ships, Third World owners and operators, different trades, even different cargoes. I missed the old days. I missed the Ellerman Company that I knew and remembered. It seemed odd for me not to be directly involved with ships as part of my life. Most of all, I missed walking up and down those gangways."

Quarters aboard Ellerman cargo liners, such as the *City of Brooklyn* of 1949, were quite typical of British ships carrying a dozen or so passengers. The ship's verandah cafe (top) included an adjacent cocktail bar; the twin-bedded stateroom (centre) had a private bathroom and forced-air ventilation; and the chief engineer's cabin (bottom) included a sitting area for entertaining. *All Cunard-Ellerman Group.*

Isthmian Spans the Globe

Saigon! Bangkok! Penang! Calcutta! Bahrein! Ras Tanura! From the sweltering Persian Gulf to the far-off Spice Islands to the hustle and bustle of Hong Kong, reports would come into the Isthmian Steamship Company offices along Lower Manhattan's 'Steamship Row' in the 1950s. Then, the Company ran over two dozen freighters on some of the most fascinating routes in the World. Eight ships maintained their around-the-World service, all sailing westbound; seven others served the Indian trade; three went to the Persian Gulf; three more went eastbound via Suez to Indonesia and Malaya; another three worked a joint service to the Hawaiian islands with the San Francisco-based Matson Line; and finally, four other ships worked an intercoastal service, shuttling between the U.S. Atlantic and Pacific Coasts via Panama.

Trim and well-maintained, Isthmian ships bore dove grey hulls, silver or brown masts and plain buff funnels. At New York Erie Basin Terminal, their homeport, they landed incredibly diverse cargoes: Outwards, Isthmian ships delivered the vast produce of post-War America: the machinery, railway equipment, generators, turbines, farm vehicles and the vast array of steel products that came from the Isthmian's parent, the United States Steel Company.

Isthmian was originally born through America's neglect of her own shipping. In the early 1900s, after a long period of decay in the American shipping industry, the United States Steel Products Company, as it then was, found itself at a serious disadvantage in the export trade. The foreign shipowners, whose vessels U.S. Steel was forced to use, had a tendency to favor the development of their own national trade. This they were able to do by giving lower freight rates to their own nationals or by refraining from giving Americans the necessary assurance of adequate transportation service to permit the Americans to enter the strongly competitive overseas market.

In 1910, as a first step toward the provision of reliable export-import transportation for its products, the steel company purchased ten cargo ships. They were placed under British registry in two newly inaugurated lines, the New York & South American Line and the Maple Leaf Line. But upon the opening of the Panama Canal in 1914, the two lines were combined under the title of Isthmian, which honored the new route across the Isthmus of Panama. At the same time, the registry of the ten ships was brought under the American flag. After the First World War, the post-War boom brought even stronger markets for Isthmian ships. Using the U.S. Steel-owned shipyards at Chickasaw, Alabama and at Kearney, New Jersey, they built 28 freighters of a special design to carry odd-shaped steel products. The ships were also given heavy-lift booms capable of hoisting up to 30 tons of steel, as well as provision to carry liquid cargoes in bulk.

By the early 1950s, Isthmian freighters were heavily booked not only with U.S. Steel cargoes but others as well. There were also comfortable quarters for 6-12 passengers on most of their ships. In 1951, a sample fare from San Francisco to Bangkok was $550 while three-months around-the-World was priced at $1,225. The movements of their fleets were certainly diverse as indicated by this partial listing of the fleet for October 11th 1950:

Steel King	Tripoli
Steel Apprentice	Beirut
Steel Age	Manila
Steel Mariner	San Francisco
Steel Ranger	Cristobal
Steel Fabricator	Calcutta
Steel Chemist	Straits of Gibraltar
Steel Director	Halifax
Steel Architect	Honolulu
Steel Recorder	New York
Steel Worker	Basrah
Steel Designer	Bombay

But as with all US-flag shipowners, operating costs were high. In the early '50s for example, the monthly wages for an 8,000-ton Isthmian freighter with a crew of 40 amounted to $21,000 per month. Similarly, wages for the same ship but under the Greek flag would be $8,300; Dutch flag, $7,600; British, $6,700; Norwegian, $6,400; and Italian, $5,400. After long struggles with both high operating costs and then foreign-flag competitors, U.S. Steel sold its Isthmian division to another American shipping company, the States Marine Lines. The two were merged for a time as the States Marine-Isthmian Agency. However, the original Isthmian fleet, which dated from 1945-46, grew older and therefore even more costly. Many finished their days on the U.S. Government's military supply runs to Southeast Asia in the late '60s before going off to Eastern scrapyards. By the early 'seventies, the Isthmian name had just about disappeared from the sealanes.

(opposite top) **A classic Wartime-built C2-type freighter, Isthmian's *Steel Rover*, was especially fitted for the transport of steel products.** *Frank O. Braynard Collection.*

(opposite) **Built in Scotland in 1950, the 8,644-ton *Eastern Queen* ran a regular service between Yokohama, Kobe, Hong Kong and the Australian ports of Sydney and Melbourne. Her cargo capacity included tanks for vegetable oils. There were very fine quarters for 26 European first class passengers along with 30 in Asiatic first class, some 200 in steerage and at least 500 as deck class for coastal sailings in the Far East. Well-known in the East, she was owned by a subsidiary of one of Hong Kong's most illustrious companies: Jardine, Matheson & Company Limited.** *Frank O. Braynard Collection.*

Crown Colony: Hong Kong

As this book goes to press in 1997 Hong Kong has just been handed back to the Chinese under a long-standing treaty. But for many years it was British-owned-although said to be the most Chinese settlement outside China itself. This territory of 391 square miles lies partly on the mainland and partly on two islands, Stonecutters' and Hong Kong. Its natural harbor could handle dozens of ocean ships at one time as well as a waterborne population of just short of 155,000 (1955) that lived on the hundreds of junks and sampans.

(above) **Ships at Hong Kong: three ships at berth are (from left to right) Eastern & Australian Line's *Aramac* (the former Cunarder *Parthia*), United Netherlands Navigation Company's *Spaarnekerk* and Hamburg America's *Rheinland*.**

In another view, one of the largest callers in the late 1950s was the 27,632-ton *Oronsay* of Britain's Orient Line.
Both photos James L. Shaw Collection.

The 7,400-ton, 1949-built *Changsha* (seen here in the shadow of Sydney Harbor Bridge) ran a passenger-cargo service between Australia, Taiwan and Hong Kong. Owned by The China Navigation Company Ltd. of London and Hong Kong, she carried over 150 passengers in two classes.
Frank O. Braynard Collection.

In the early '60s, China's largest passenger ship was the British-built *Guanghua*, which was used mostly for coastal services. She had been the *Highland Princess* of 1930, a ship long used on Royal Mail Lines' London-East Coast of South America run.
Alex Duncan.

The 3,100-ton *Kimanis*, owned by Singapore's Straits Steamship Company, was one of a series of unusual-looking ships specially designed for the trade between Singapore and Borneo.
C. B. Mulholland.

Another small passenger-cargo ship was the Dutch-flag *Sinabang*, pictured in Sydney Harbor, which sailed on the Royal Interocean Lines' run to Indonesia. *Frank O. Braynard Collection.*

Chapter Five
Pacific Waters

President Liners to the Orient

For several decades, the American President Lines of San Francisco was one of America's finest and best known passenger-cruise companies. Expectedly, they were particularly popular on the West Coast where their ships were just about household names. Great advertisements themed to 'President liners to the Orient' regularly filled the pages of *Holiday* and *National Geographic*.

Still in business, but now only in container-cargo shipping, American President's roots go back to 1901. Then, the Dollar Steamship Company was formed, using a 200-ton steam schooner, the *Newsboy*, to ferry lumber around the Pacific Northwest. Quickly, the Company prospered and expanded and then, after the First World War, acquired a good number of surplus passenger ships. All were given President names and one of them, the *President Harrison*, inaugurated one of the Company's trademark services, four-month around-the-World voyages, in January 1924. Minimum fares were then $900!

The original Dollar Company collapsed in 1938, but was then restructured financially as American President. In the post-Second World War years, the Company ran three splendid liners: the sisters *President Cleveland* and *President Wilson*, and later the *President Roosevelt*. There were six-week cruises by the late 1960s to Alaska, Mexico, the Caribbean and even as far afield as Scandinavia and the Mediterranean. World voyages continued with regularity until 1965, using the 96-passenger sisterships *President Monroe* and *President Polk* which also had a good cargo capacity.

When P*resident Cleveland* left San Francisco on her final cruise in 1972, it was also the end of American President liner services (their 12-passenger freighters did continue for some years thereafter, however). Simply, it had become too expensive and uncompetitive to operate US-flag liners.

By the 1990s, American President was mega-container-ships. The latest generation, flying the flag of the Marshall Islands, has even dropped the Presidential nomenclature. The ships now bear names such as *APL Japan*, *APL Korea* and *APL Singapore*.

One of the Wartime-built C3-class freighters, the *President McKinley*, is shown unloading some of the earliest containers at Los Angeles docks. The date is 1966. *Frank O. Braynard Collection.*

While American President maintained well-known trans-Pacific and North American intercoastal services, their most famous operation was their around-the-World service. Beginning at the US East Coast, the ships passed through Panama and then called at California before continuing to the Far East, Southeast Asia, India, the Suez Canal and the Mediterranean heading home. Certainly, diverse cargoes filled the holds of the ships in this service, but it was also very appealing to passengers, especially those wanting a three-month circum-navigation. The 1940-built *President Polk* (top) and her twin sister, the *President Monroe*, were special in that they had very spacious accommodations for as many as 96 passengers, all in first class. Twelve-passenger freighters filled out the remainder of the global schedule, but especially popular were the altered Mariner Class ships such as the 9,200-ton *President Coolidge* (above). Large and fast for her time (the 1950s and early '60s), she had extremely luxurious quarters for her dozen passengers. Amenities included a top-deck observation lounge and a passenger elevator. *Alex Duncan.*

Liners at Honolulu

"Back in the 1930s, when I was a youngster in Honolulu, the great ocean liners and cruiseships came and went with almost daily regularity. We would go down to the Aloha Tower Pier and look up at these huge ships, some of the largest then afloat. They were certainly amongst the most palatial." Eric Newman still lives in the Honolulu area and still watches the cruise liners when they visit. Some time ago, we were shipmates, but in far different waters, in the Mediterranean, on a cruise out of Venice onboard the *Crystal Harmony*.

"I see the *Constitution*★ and the *Independence* of American Hawaii Cruises almost every Saturday," he then said. "They are classic liners in exterior design. They each have two big stacks, which of course remind me of those bygone years, the golden era. Back in the '30s, we had the American-flag ships of the Matson Line, the Dollar Line and later the American President Lines. Then there were the Canadian Pacific Empress liners and the ships of Japan's NYK Line. We would also have the once-a-year visits of the around-the-World cruiseships – the *Empress of Britain*, the *Reliance*, the *Franconia* and the little *Stella Polaris*."

Immediately after the Second World War, Honolulu harbor continued to welcome passenger vessels but there were far more troopships than actual luxury liners. Regular, peacetime commercial service reopened gradually with Matson's *Lurline* in 1948. That same year, American President added its new post-War liners, the *President Cleveland* and the *President Wilson*. Canadian Pacific did not, however, resume its trans-Pacific passenger service and for the most part, the Japanese were out as well.

"By the late 1950s and '60s, Honolulu was once again a busy passenger and cruise port," according to Mr. Newman. "American President and Matson had expanded with ships like the *President Roosevelt* and *Matsonia*, *Mariposa* and *Monterey*. But England's P&O-Orient Lines had arrived as well. They had about a dozen big liners that called regularly – with names like *Orsova* and *Arcadia*, *Canberra* and *Oriana*. They might be coming or going to Australia, Vancouver and California or across to Japan. The jumbo jets still hadn't made an impact and so these great, two-class ships were busy, profitable links. You could go all the way to London or Cape Town or completely around-the-World from Honolulu. In a very simple tourist class cabin, you could travel for as little as $10 a day in the early '60s. And of course, lots of tourists came from the US mainland by sea, stayed in hotels and then went back by a later sailing or by air."

Today, the services of Matson, American President and P&O-Orient are gone. With the exception of the afore-mentioned *Independence*, regular services are run only by airlines. "But we still have some special visitors – the *QE2*, the *Rotterdam*, the *Royal Viking Sun* and others," added Eric Newman. "Once, about twenty-five years ago, even the *Leonardo Da Vinci* made a special call. I've been watching the liners at Honolulu for some sixty years and the sight of them is still a great treat."

★The *Constitution* has since been withdrawn but the *Independence* sails on.

The 1931-built *Lurline* was Matson's most popular and perhaps most profitable ship in the 1950s. Used on the California-Hawaii passenger run, she carried over 30,000 passengers in 1950 and contributed almost 15% of the Matson Line's profits in that same year. In 1957, she was joined by a pre-War sister, the *Monterey*, which was reconditioned as the *Matsonia*. *James L. Shaw Collection*.

To run its South Seas-Australia service, Matson bought two Mariner Class freighters in the mid '50s and had them rebuilt as 365-passenger cruiseships, the *Mariposa* and *Monterey* (shown passing under the Golden Gate Bridge at San Francisco). Their six-week voyages were particularly popular with a roundtrip clientele who began to come year after year. *Matson Lines.*

Matson also ran a sizeable freighter fleet to Hawaii as well as the South Pacific. In the early 1950s, some of their C3-Class freighters such as the *Hawaiian Planter* were run in coordinated schedules with another American shipowner, the Isthmian Lines.
Frank O. Braynard Collection.

Denmark's biggest shipowner, the Maersk Line, ran scheduled services to the Far East and Southeast Asia, both from Europe as well as US ports. In this view, the 6,600-ton, 1949-built *Anna Maersk* prepares for a voyage to the Orient. Shown at Norfolk, she is across the shed from an Isthmian Line freighter, the *Steel King*, which is destined for the Middle East by way of Suez. *Frank O. Braynard Collection.*

The New York-based Isbrandtsen Company ran a fleet of two dozen cargo liners on services around the World. (opposite page top) The C2-Class freighter *Flying Enterprise II* loads cargo at Long Beach, California for the Company's Far East service, calling at Manila, Hong Kong, Shanghai, Pusan, Kobe and Yokohama. Meanwhile, (left) another 12-passenger C2-type freighter, the *Flying Eagle*, passes through the Panama Canal. She was used in the same Far Eastern service, but from New York and other US East Coast ports. Passage rates in the early '50s from New York to Hong Kong were set at $550. (opposite page bottom) The *Flying Endeavor*, shown departing from New York, was used in the Company's 90-day around-the-World service, calling at Genoa, Alexandria, Karachi, Bombay, Singapore, Manila, Hong Kong, Kobe and Yokohama. There were two sailings per month from New York and the full voyage was priced at $950 in 1953. (below) One of the Company's Victory Class freighters, the 7,600-ton *Brooklyn Heights*, is shown entering Hong Kong. She carried 12 male passengers, all in dormitory-style accommodations.

All Frank O. Braynard Collection.

The American Pioneer Line, a division of the United States Lines, had a strong place in Pacific cargo shipping in the 1950s and '60s. One of their C2-Class freighters, the *Pioneer Glen* (above), was used in their 'Down Under' service to Australia and New Zealand. The larger, faster *Pioneer Moor* (left), a Mariner Class freighter built in 1953, worked with her seven sisters on the US-Far East run. While ships such as the *Pioneer Glen* later finished their days at the breakers, the *Pioneer Moor* was converted to a containership in 1970.
Frank O. Braynard Collection & Alex Duncan.

Japanese-flag trans-Pacific services resumed gradually in the early 1950s. One of the first ships on the revived New York run was the *London Maru*, shown here at New York on April 8th 1954. She is berthed across from Isthmian Line's *Steel Fabricator*.
Frank O. Braynard Collection.

An established pre-War Japanese service to the East Coast of South America was resumed in 1952. Carrying cargo as well as many migrants in third class accommodations, this service employed five combination passenger-cargo ships. In this aerial view at Yokohama, the new *Brazil Maru* is departing with the converted *Santos Maru* in the background. The former was completed in 1954, the latter refitted from 12-passenger freighter service.
Hisashi Noma Collection.

The Japanese were busily rebuilding their vast merchant fleet by the late 1950s as well as resuming their trade with foreign shipowners. In this quite active aerial view of the Yokohama Ocean Terminal, no less than 5 ships can be seen. At the top of the outer dock is a Daido Line freighter then being used on the Panama Canal/New York service. Just beyond, the passenger-cargo liner *Brazil Maru* is departing for ports along the East Coast of South America. Her accommodations included third class quarters for as many as 900 Japanese migrants going to new lives in Brazil and Argentina. Just aft of her is another passenger-cargo ship with migrant facilities, the *Santos Maru*. On the inner side at the top is a Wilh. Wilhelmsen Line freighter and then NYK Line's *Akagi Maru*, then one of the largest and fastest ships serving on the Japanese-US East Coast run.
Hisashi Noma Collection.

In another view, at Philadelphia in the early 1950s, the Mitsui-OSK Line freighter *Africa Maru* arrives from Japanese ports via Panama. An 8,300-ton vessel, she was built to carry 12 cabin passengers as a cargo ship, but was later enlarged with austere quarters for some 524 migrants and thereafter used on the Japan-East Coast of South America trade.
Hisashi Noma Collection.

Chapter Six
Oil

A Precious Cargo

By 1960, one out of every five ships was a tanker. This specialized fleet had more than doubled since the beginning of the Second World War. These ships ranged in size from coastal vessels of a mere few hundred tons to the classic T-2 tankers of World War Two at 9,000 tons to 50,000-tonners by 1960 and later to 100,000 and 200,000-ton ships. The larger ships, say from 20,000 tons upwards, are usually engaged in hauling crude petroleum from the World's oil-producing areas to seaboard refineries; smaller tankers carry refined products to distribution centers up and down coasts and into inland waterways.

The first ship built exclusively to carry petroleum was the *Gluckauf*, launched in 1886. She was the prototype of the present day tanker with engine room and funnel placed aft. One of the problems faced by her designers was the obvious danger that her liquid cargo, while sloshing about in heavy seas, might capsize the vessel. Therefore, the *Gluckauf* and her oil-carrying successors had to be compartmentalized. The hulls of modern tankers are honeycombed with athwartship bulkheads, which divide their cargo space into main tanks, which, in turn, are subdivided by fore-and-aft longitudinal bulkheads.

Large tankers remain very efficient carriers, especially when it is considered that one-half of most voyages are made in ballast. In the early 1960s, the American-flag Sun Oil Company estimated that it cost approximately one cent per gallon to transport oil from a Texas oil field to their refinery near Philadelphia in tankers such as their *Western Sun*, which had a capacity of 10,500,000 gallons.

The French-flag *Ardeshir* was a typical T2-Class tanker, of which US shipyards produced hundreds during the Second World War. Many of these found their way under foreign registry soon after the War ended.
Frank O. Braynard Collection.

Larger, faster, more efficient tankers began to appear in the late 1940s. The 628-foot long *Esso New York* was commissioned in 1950 and had a tank capacity of 230,000 barrels or just over 9,600,000 gallons. One of eleven sisters built for Esso Standard Oil Company of New York, she had a service speed of 16 knots and carried a crew of 40. *Frank O. Braynard Collection.*

A Cities Service tanker, the 10,449-ton *Bents Fort*, passes under the Bear Mountain Bridge, near West Point, New York and along the Hudson River. The 524-footer, shown in June 1952, had delivered a cargo of refined petroleum products to the Cities Service Marine Terminal at Rennsselaer, just across from Albany. The entire cargo amounted to 140,000 barrels. *Frank O. Braynard Collection.*

Tankers take heavy beatings in storms with waves frequently washing across the decks because of the low freeboard. (above) The *Western Sun*, owned by the Sun Oil Company, is smashed by a heavy wave in a gale off Cape Hatteras, Virginia. (opposite) Socony Mobil's *Socony-Vacuum* rides low in the water on a voyage from Beaumont, Texas to Providence, Rhode Island.
Both Frank O. Braynard Collection.

One of the more unusual speciality tankers was the US-flag *Angelo Petri*. Trading between the three coasts of the United States, this 17,000-tonner carried a special cargo: wine. *Frank O. Braynard Collection.*

By the mid 1950s, demands on tankers became more and more pressing. There was a need for larger capacities. But rather than build new tonnage, some companies decided to enlarge existing vessels in a process known as 'jumboizing'. In March 1957, the Gulf Oil Corporation's twelve-year-old *Gulfmeadows* is being transformed at the Bethlehem Steel Shipyards at Baltimore, Maryland. First, the original deck housing is shifted to the new mid-body (opposite bottom). Then heavily ballasted, the stern section is detached as the original mid-section and bow are floated out in preparation for the insertion of the new mid-body with deck housing (above). The 14½-knot tanker was extended from 524 to 572 feet and from 10,200 gross tons to 19,900 tons. Upon completion, she took on a new name as well: *Gulfbeaver*. *Frank O. Braynard Collection.*

The size of tankers grew steadily. When completed in 1953, the 27,853-ton *Tina Onassis* (above) , shown in the Sturrock Graving Dock at Cape Town, ranked as one of the largest tankers afloat. The 776-footer, near to the length of such liners as the *Mauretania* and *Ile De France*, was owned by the Greek Onassis Group, but flew the Liberian colors. Within five years, such ships as the *Harold H. Helm*, at 51,300 tons and 885 feet in length, topped the tanker record list. A decade later, in 1968, the record went to such ships as the *Universe Ireland*. She had a tonnage of 149,600 and a length of 1,133 feet.

(opposite page) In this comparative view at the Bethlehem Steel Shipyard at Baltimore, we see the 18,700-ton, 645-foot *Gulfspray* which was considered a large tanker when she was completed in 1960. A decade or so later, the 60,000-ton, 883-foot *Arco Anchorage* was already rather average. *Frank O. Braynard Collection.*

Chapter Seven
Special Ships, Special Cargoes

In the 1950s, ship designers and shipbuilders became increasingly involved in creating special-purpose ships to carry particular types of cargo. Most of these special cargoes were commodities which lent themselves to bulk handling in large amounts. For example, there was a rapid rise in the number of ore and bauxite carriers – big, deep-hulled ships that can carry 60,000 tons and more of ore from remote areas to the World's steel and aluminium manufacturing centers. Along with car-carriers, container-carriers, wine-carriers and even orange-juice carriers, there were the ships of Britain's Bowater Paper Company. Their speciality cargo was pulp and newsprint, and they ran between Eastern Canada and the United States and Northern Europe.

Two thousand five hundred Liberty Ships like the *Joseph Lee*, shown offloading at London while sailing under Lykes Line management for the U.S. Maritime Commission, were mass-produced in American yards during the War. Their class letters were EC-2, standing for Emergency Cargo Ships between 400-450 feet long. The standard length of an 11-knot Liberty was 441 feet. Liberty ships served under a wide variety of flags until the 1960s. Few were still sailing commercially by the 1970s and there were practically none at all by the '80s. The *Joseph Lee* herself endured until the Fall of 1964, when she was broken-up at Portland, Oregon. *Stan Rawlings.*

Two of Bowater's green-hulled ships are shown here. The *Constance Bowater* is on the left while the slightly larger *Sarah Bowater*, heavily laden, is in mid-stream. This view dates from 1959.
Frank O. Braynard Collection.

Heavy Lift

Norway's Christen Smith Line was noted for its heavy-lift freighters. They handled some of the World's heaviest and bulkiest cargoes. In this view, dating from 1955, two Christen Smith vessels are taking on railway locomotives that are bound for Arabian ports. Seen at the Erie Railroad's heavy cargo terminal at Weehawken, New Jersey, the *Christen Smith* is on the outer berth; the *Beljeanne* behind her. The locomotives were handled not only by the heavy-lift booms onboard the two ships, but also by a trio of 50-ton Erie cranes along the dockside. *Frank O. Braynard Collection.*

On another occasion, the freighter *Colebrooke* is discharging a heavy load, which is being handled by the 200-ton crane at Stormont Wharf at Belfast.
Frank O. Braynard Collection.

In the Brooklyn docks at New York, heavy cargo is being handled by one of the port's floating cranes, the steam-powered *Century*. Placed between a cargo barge and the ship herself, the crane's boom could swing into position to handle bulky goods. The *Century* had a capacity of 175 tons, the greatest of all the floating derricks in New York harbor in the 1950s and '60s.
Frank O. Braynard Collection.

Converted from a more conventional C4-Class cargo ship, the *USNS Pvt. Leonard C. Brostrom* was one of the mightiest ships under the US flag in the 1950s. Converted in 1954 for the Military Sea Transportation Service, she had single boom lifts of as much as 150 tons at the hook. That huge lifting capacity, then the largest of any ship under the US flag, freed the 520-foot long ship from dependence on shoreside facilities. Her lifting abilities were especially useful for the handling of such cumbersome cargoes as locomotives and large cannons. Her sister was the *USNS Marine Fiddler*. *Frank O. Braynard Collection.*

Freighters on the North American Great Lakes were a distinctive breed: long and low with the engines and therefore funnels placed far aft. The wheelhouses were placed far forward. In this view, taken at Buffalo in March 1954, there are no less than 5 'ore carriers' being prepared after a long winter lay-up for further service on 'the Lakes'. *Frank O. Braynard Collection.*

Prior to the opening of the St Lawrence Seaway in 1959, only small freighters could travel beyond the St Lawrence River and into the North American Great Lakes. These services were available, however, only in the ice-free months from April through November. Ships were then detoured to ports in the Canadian Maritimes, where their cargoes were transshipped by rail, or to other services such as the US Gulf Coast.

The Swedish Chicago Line's *Monica Smith* sailed between Northern Europe and the Great Lakes. She would load American-made manufactured goods at such ports as Cleveland, Detroit, Chicago, Milwaukee and Duluth before returning to Copenhagen and Gothenburg.

Frank O. Braynard Collection.

Ore-carriers continued to grow in size and capacity in the 1950s. In this view from August 1951, the 9,125-ton Swedish *Rautas* is offloading 12,000 tons of high grade ore at the Baltimore & Ohio Railroad's new terminal at Baltimore. Two 15-ton shovels, one in each tower, bit into her cargo, which was then transshipped to major US steel centers. In the early '50s, there was an increasing flow of foreign ores into the United States from such places as Liberia, Venezuela, Chile and Cuba. At this facility, the twin unloading machines had a sustained capacity of 2,000 tons per hour, which meant they could discharge a ship such as the *Rautas* in six hours. *Frank O. Braynard Collection.*

(opposite top) **The transport of automobiles became increasingly important in the 1950s. The 1943-built** *Empire Celtic*, **a former World War II tank landing ship, was later renamed** *Celtic Ferry* **and was redesigned to transport military vehicles and commercial cars. In this view from April 1950, she is loaded with 142 cars and trucks (half on deck, half in the hold below) for another run between London and Antwerp. That year, Britain exported by sea some 258,000 cars and 93,000 commercial vehicles.** *Frank O. Braynard Collection.*

(opposite) **Sweden's Wallenius Lines, who name their ships after operas, are well known for their auto-carriers. The first Wallenius vessel to be specially built for the purpose, in 1955, was the** *Rigoletto*. **Today, the likes of 950-foot long Japanese car-carriers can transport over 6,000 automobiles at one time.** *James L. Shaw Collection.*

The *Seatrain Georgia*, shown arriving on her maiden voyage at Edgewater, New Jersey in 1951, was one of six sisters and near-sisters designed to carry 100 loaded freight cars on a mile of standard gauge tracks along her decks. She also had a liquid capacity of 12,000 barrels. Seatrain Lines operated a coastwise service between New York and such ports as Savannah, New Orleans, Texas City and Galveston. The large crane behind the ship handled the freight cars. While Seatrain later abandoned its railway-ship system (in the early 1970s), that enormous Edgewater crane remained in situ for some years until dismantled in 1985. *Frank O. Braynard Collection.*

The first cargo containers in the United States were carried on a converted T2-type tanker, the *Ideal X*, in 1954. Innovative and efficient, it soon led the Pan-Atlantic Steamship Company, a forerunner to the Sea-Land

Service Corporation, to convert no less than six ships in 1957-58. One of these predecessors to the pure container ships of the 1960s was the C2-type freighter *Iberville*, which had been completed in April 1943 as a 1,300-troop capacity transport. After the War, she sailed as a commercial freighter for the Waterman Steamship Company. In December 1957, she was selected for conversion to the container-ship *Gateway City* (seen here). This process included the extension of her beam by 11 feet through the fitting of sponsons on the midbody section. In addition, two gantry cranes, one foreward and the other aft, were installed for the handling of a maximum of 226 containers. Overall, the 6,900-ton ship increased in tonnage to 9,000. Long used in the US coastal and Caribbean trades, the *Gateway City* was laid-up for a time before being scrapped in Hong Kong in 1978. *Frank O. Braynard Collection.*

Chapter Eight
Shipbuilding

Britain was the shipbuilding center of the world in the 1950s. This busy scene at Sunderland shows a variety of ships being fitted-out and undergoing repair as well as the freighter *Granwood* being towed to a fitting-out berth. *Frank O. Braynard Collection.*

The tanker *Border Keep*, owned by Lowland Tanker Co. and managed by Britain's Common Brothers Limited, goes down the ways in 1953. The 11,000-tonner, built by Blythswood Shipbuilding in Scotland, could handle oil cargo in any part of the World. *Frank O. Braynard Collection.*

World Shipbuilding 1953

country	ships	gross tonnage
Great Britain	587	5,546,182
Sweden	152	1,466,202
Germany	176	1,438,686
Holland	138	1,121,626
United States	57	823,645
France	69	772,029
Japan	55	578,640
Norway	73	575,316
Italy	29	379,088
Belgium	28	309,448
Denmark	44	268,400
Spain	31	156,986
Canada	13	121,200
Australia	15	66,588
India	9	45,400
Hong Kong	4	11,600
Turkey	1	3,800

Source: *Shipbuilders Council of America*

Shaw, Savill Line's 20,000-ton *Southern Cross*, the first really large liner to have her engines and funnel mounted aft, is being moved to the fitting-out berth at Harland & Wolff's Belfast yard after being launched by Queen Elizabeth II in August 1954. *James L. Shaw Collection.*

Another liner, the Grace Line's 300-passenger *Santa Rosa*, goes down the ways on August 28th 1957 at the Newport News Shipyard in Virginia. *Grace Line.*

The 46,000-ton tanker *Capiluna*, owned by the Hercules Tankers Corporation, is almost ready for launching in 1960 at the Bethlehem Steel Shipyard at Quincy, Massachusetts. In this case, however, the dock containing the 736-footer will be flooded and then the ship will sail out. *Frank O. Braynard Collection.*

Following the destruction of the Second World War and then the strict Allied controls of the late 1940s, the Japanese shipbuilding industry resurfaced by the '50s. In this view, dated June 18, 1958, all slipways at Mitsubishi's Nagasaki yard are occupied. By the late 1960s, the Japanese would be the leading shipbuilders in the World and would have the distinction of having the World's largest ships, virtual fleets of supertankers. *Hisashi Noma Collection.*

Merchant Fleets of the World 1952

country	ships	gross tonnage
United States	3,441	25,627,000
British Empire	3,006	18,797,000
Norway	961	5,533,000
Sweden	594	2,157,000
France	559	3,276,000
Panama	550	3,730,000
Italy	517	3,048,000

Source: *US Department of Commerce*

One of the great shipbuilding projects of the late 1950s was the construction of the World's longest liner, the 1,035-foot long *France*. Built at the Chantiers de l'Atlantique yard at St. Nazaire, France, she took 4 years, 3 months and 28 days to complete. Her first steel plates were laid in place in October 1957. Some weighing as much as 50 tons, they came from such French cities as Orléans, Le Havre, Lyons, Grenoble and Lille. Fitting them into place was akin to a giant jigsaw puzzle.

She was launched on May 11th 1960. A day later some 2,000 technicians invaded the 66,000-ton liner to begin the finishing touches. That summer, her rudder and four propeller shafts were installed. It took three weeks to fit the giant 74-ton rudder and the 60-foot long shafts, the longest in the World. There were also 18,000 miles of wiring, 1,300 telephones and 28 miles of ventilating lines.

Three views of the *France's* construction: (below) **the great hull just months before launching.**
Richard Faber Collection.

(right) **The mighty, curved bow section.**
Richard Faber Collection.

(bottom) **Finally, at the fitting out berth at St Nazaire, the new flagship of the French merchant marine as she appeared in the Fall of 1961.**
Fred Rodriguez Collection.

Repairs to ocean ships could vary from a few hours at a shipyard to a few months. Refits and annual overhauls tended to be planned well in advance, but then emergencies required sudden and prompt attention. This often meant work going on well into the night or on weekends and holidays – even Christmas Day, sometimes. In this view from the early 1950s, the US Army troop transport *George W. Goethals* enters the Todd shipyard at Brooklyn, New York for quick, but urgent repairs to her propeller. So sudden was the need before the ship sailed across the North Atlantic to Bremerhaven that the 352 wives and children of American overseas servicemen stayed aboard. With an around-the-clock crew attending to the 492-foot long ship's needs, she was ready to sail within 48 hours. In another scene, the Glasgow registered Liberty ship *Marabank* is far from home as she undergoes repairs in the big Sturrock Graving Dock at Cape Town. The Bank Line ship has had her propeller removed. *Frank O. Braynard Collection.*

Ship repair at Hoboken, New Jersey: United Fruit's *Comayagua* is shown high-and-dry in a view dating from 1954. Her hull is being sandblasted and repainted in a new coat of heat-resistant white. The white reflected the sun's rays, especially in tropical Caribbean and Central American ports, and thereby reduced stress on the ships refrigeration and cooling systems. The 7,075-ton *Comayagua* could transport 78,000 bunches of bananas on a single voyage. During this period, she remained at the Bethlehem Steel yard for nearly fourteen days. *Frank O. Braynard Collection.*

In another view from Hoboken, dating from September 1962, the 630-foot long containership *San Juan* is being readied for her first voyage. She had been at the shipyard for over six months. She was converted from a 520-foot tanker, a job which involved the replacement of her original midbody section with a new 417-foot midbody that was actually 10 feet wider than the original. Intended for Sea-Land's intracoastal service between the US East and West Coasts via the Caribbean and the Panama Canal, the rebuilt ship – one of the earliest in the then new 'container generation' – was equipped with her own lifting gear for the handling of her containerized cargo. *Frank O. Braynard Collection.*

Chapter Nine

The End of the Line

The 5,000-ton freighter *Flying Enterprise*, owned by the Isbrandtsen Line of New York, made international news when she was lost in early 1952. She had left Hamburg on December 21st, carrying 10 passengers and general cargo which included nearly 1,300 tons of pig iron and 900 tons of coffee. On the 28th, she was caught in a severe cyclonic storm some 500 miles west of Fastnet. She radioed that she had a 30 degree list to port, a crack across the deck and was just drifting. She soon gave out an SOS signal. Another freighter, the *Southland*, later took off most of the passengers and crew. Still later, the American troopship *General A.W. Greely* took off the remainder with the sole exception of the master, Captain Kurt Carlsen. He stood by as the *Flying Enterprise*, which was now listing at 60 degrees and rolling to 80 degrees and in worsening weather, awaited the arrival of the salvage tug. Captain Carlsen spent 4 days and nights aboard his badly battered vessel. Attempts to tow her later failed and Carlsen eventually had to leave before she sank on January 10th, just 62 miles from Falmouth. The devotion of her Master to his ship and her owners endures as a heroic act of seamanship. *Laurence Dunn Collection.*

After certainly one of the most notorious accidents of her time, the Swedish passenger-cargo liner *Stockholm* returned to New York missing a good part of her raked bow section following a collision with the Italian liner *Andrea Doria*. There were 51 casualties in the July 1956 disaster, which occurred in thick fog off the New England coast. The *Andrea Doria* sank and the 525-foot long *Stockholm* later spent almost five months at a Brooklyn shipyard having a new bow section fitted. *Flying Camera.*

Fire is, of course, a potent and dramatic ending for any ship. The Argentine combo ship *Rio Jachal* caught fire while lying at her New York pier in September 1962. The blaze spread quickly through her passenger accommodations and sent clouds of smoke drifting across the Hudson River to New Jersey. Fireboats, Coast Guard craft and tugs were called in to assist. Expectedly, the next outward sailing for the twelve-year-old ship was cancelled and instead she was laid-up at a Brooklyn shipyard. Little was done. The 550-foot long ship was eventually returned to Buenos Aires and repaired, but burned again before finally being laid-up permanently and then scrapped in 1970. *Frank O. Braynard Collection.*

The Idle Fleet

They sit nested together in rows, a dozen or so ships in each. They are roped and chained together. In the late 1980s, there were about 8 separate groupings and altogether nearly 140 ships. It was, in fact, the largest organized 'idle fleet' in the world. It belonged to the US Government, the so-called 'defense fleet', located in Virginia's James River and just off Fort Eustis, which is upriver from busy Norfolk and Newport News.

Poetically, these ships sit in 'silent abandonement'. They are not, however, completely abandoned, even if their most regular visitors are the birds that rest on their foredecks. There is a shoreside crew of about 200 to look after them, using workboats, tugs, barges and even a heavy-lift crane that fitted aboard the *Manchester*, a former cable-layer. Looking from the shore, the ships are neatly grouped, securely anchored in the mud and silt. Almost entirely empty (except possibly for some storage items, such as lifeboats stowed in their holds), they sit quite high

in the water and consequently appear larger, even mightier. Many of them, especially the freighters, still wear the commercial funnel markings of the otherwise vanished likes of the Grace, Moore-McCormack, American Export and United States lines. They have names such as *Santa Lucia* and *Santa Elena*, *Mormacdawn* and *Mormacmoon*, *Export Courier* and *Export Agent*, the *American Challenger* and *American Ranger*.

At its peak, just after the Second World War, there were 600 ships moored in this James River fleet. Then, there were also 8 other such fleets including one along the upper Hudson River, about forty miles from New York City. It was said then that America had more ships in 'mothballs' than most other countries had in actual service. Today, with far fewer ships, there are only two other fleets, at Beaumont, Texas and Suisun Bay, California. There are, however, a number of 'outpost ships', one or more vessels kept in reserve status at a dozen or so ports such as Jacksonville, Norfolk and Baltimore. Most of these as well as the 40 or so specially designated ships in the Virginia fleet are part of the US Government's 'ready reserve'. They can be activated, should an emergency arise (such as the Gulf War in 1991), in 5-10 days. Others can be prepared in three or four weeks.

Among the older ships, there has been some house-cleaning underway. Much of the remaining Second World War tonnage was being sold for scrap in the late 1980s. According to Anthony Schiavone, superintendent of the James River fleet, "We are presently [1988] selling off most of our remaining Victory ships [7,600-ton freighters built in '44-45]. The scrappers, the Taiwanese and the Spanish and later the Turks, offered about $500,000 per ship. American shipbreakers, once located at former shipyard facilities at Kearny, New Jersey; Brownsville, Texas; and San Pedro, California, can no longer compete and have all but disappeared completely."

"Our biggest sale ever was for a 60,000-ton gas carrier, the *El Paso Columbia*, which was sold to the Taiwanese for $1.6 million [also in 1988]. In addition, it cost $1.2 million for the four-month tow out across the Pacific. She had to go completely around South America because she was too wide to pass through the Panama Canal. Otherwise, it is all rather ironic. We sold Victory ships, for example, to the Spanish for scrapping, who then sold the dismantled remains to the Norwegians, who in turn recycled them into steel rods. Sometimes these new products would be sent by freighter to the Norfolk docks, within miles of the Reserve Fleet where the process first began. The rods were then resold within the United States."

Superintendent Schiavone also added, "The ships are always towed to the breakers and often as many as four leave at one time, but under the care of a single tug. They are towed in formation, each having a separate towline. Once, however, in November 1985, a Victory ship and a C2-type freighter were being towed across the mid-Atlantic when they were caught in a bad storm. The towlines snapped and the first ship rammed into the second ship. One ship sank and later the other ran aground in the Azores."

Along with the Wartime hospital ship *Sanctuary* and a number of freighters that carried a dozen or so passengers (and often in very luxurious quarters), only four passenger-troopships remained in the James River Fleet by the late '80s. Built in 1944-45, these twin-funnel ships – the *General Simon Buckner, General Alexander M. Patch, General Nelson M. Walker* and *General Maurice Rose* – were then slated for disposal as well. After World War II, these ships had been operated by MSTS, the Military Sea Transportation Service, carrying as many as 4,000 servicemen, their families, other dependents and even refugees on the North Atlantic (usually between New York and such ports as Southampton, Bremerhaven and Rota in Spain) and also across the Pacific (mostly to Yokohama, Pusan and Subic Bay in the Philippines). These Generals, along with almost all other American peacetime transports, were decommissioned in the early 'seventies. Thereafter, they too joined the 'idle fleet'.

The 17,900-ton *General W. H. Gordon* once carried as many as 4,000 servicemen and other passengers on each sailing. Built at the end of the War, in 1944, she spent the late 1960s in mothballs in the Hudson River Reserve Fleet, north of New York City. But in 1969, as the fleet was being disbanded, she was, as seen here, towed to the James River group in Virginia. Once there, she sat in silence for another twenty years until, in 1987, she was sold to Taiwanese shipbreakers. *Frank O. Braynard Collection.*

Long finished with her duties in last years of the Second World War, the Liberty ship *Mary Patten* spent twenty-five years in the James River Fleet before being towed to Spanish breakers at Castellon in the Fall of 1972. In a view from the early 1960s, seven C4-type troop transports are moored together in the foreground. Included in the next grouping are three former Moore McCormack passenger liners – the *Uruguay*, *Argentina* and *Brazil*. *both photographs: US Department of Commerce.*

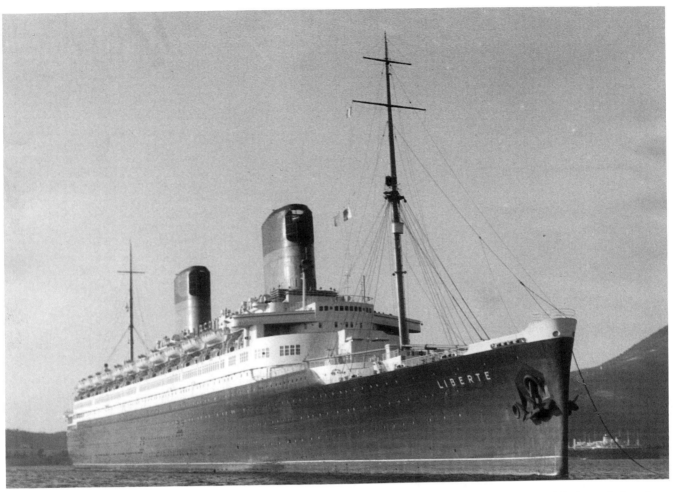

While Japanese and Hong Kong shipbreakers garnered their share of old passenger ships bound for the scrapheap, European yards were kept busy as well. Facilities at La Spezia in Italy were among the most active. Months apart in 1962, two veteran liners arrived to meet their end. The 936-foot long *Liberté* is shown on February 17th, about to drop anchor and then welcome the contingent with their acetylene torches. Her last remains would be finally hauled ashore that summer. Built in 1930, she had been the German record-breaker *Europa* and then sailed for the French Line from 1950 until her last crossing in November 1961. Another former French Line ship, the *De Grasse* of 1924, arrived at La Spezia the following summer but as the Italian *Venezuela*. She had stranded at Cannes and was considered uneconomic to repair. She had also served (1953-56) as Canadian Pacific's *Empress of Australia*.

Richard Faber Collection & Frank O. Braynard Collection.

Already stripped of her lifeboats and some of her other exterior fittings, the Union-Castle liner *Warwick Castle* is shown awaiting the demolition crews at Mihara at Hiroshima, Japan in 1960. Exactly thirty years old, she had served on the UK-South Africa mail run as well as being a trooper during the Second World War. A 20,000-tonner with accommodations for approximately 750 passengers plus considerable cargo, she had just been displaced within the Union-Castle fleet by a brand new, 37,600-ton *Windsor Castle*. The 657-foot long *Warwick Castle* was dismantled in less than six months. *Hisashi Noma Collection.*

Perhaps the most dramatic and saddening demise of a ship in those years following the Second World War was the dismantling of the great French liner *Normandie*. The 1,028-foot long luxury liner had burned at her New York City pier on February 9, 1942 while being converted to a wartime troopship. Overloaded with fire-fighters' water, she quickly capsized and then went through a costly, cumbersome salvage that took fifteen months. The 83,400-ton ship was then laid-up until declared surplus by the US Government in 1946. She was then only eleven years old.

(opposite page bottom) **Shown in this November 1946 view and rusty and scarred and shorn of her superstructure, the *Normandie* was a pitiful sight as she was towed across Lower New York Bay, under the Bayonne Bridge (in the background) and brought to a Newark, New Jersey scrapyard. She had been sold to them for a mere $161,000. The ship's proud name can be faintly seen, near her bow.** *Frank Cronican Collection.*

(above) **In the Summer of 1947, the wrecking of the *Normandie* was nearing completion. Little more than a skeleton of what was once the world's most luxurious ocean liner remains. Pieces of the $60 million ship are going into railway gondola cars located along the pierside.** *Frank Cronican Collection.*

Bibliography

Braynard, Frank O. *By Their Works Ye Shall Know Them.* New York: Gibbs & Cox Co, 1968.

Bunker, John G. *Harbor & Haven: An Illustrated History of the Port of New York.*
Woodland Hills, California: Windsor Publications, 1979.

Crowdy, Michael (editor). *Marine News (1964-1995).* Kendal, Cumbria: World Ship Society.

Devol, George (editor), *Ocean & Cruise News (1980-1995).* Stamford, Connecticut: World Ocean & Cruise Society.

Eisele, Peter & Rau, William (editors). *Steamboat Bill (1966-1995).*
New York: Steamship Historical Society of America Inc.

Hornsby, David. *Ocean Ships.* London: Ian Allan Ltd, 1982.

Kludas, Arnold. *Great Passenger Ships of the World, Volumes 1-5.* Cambridge, England: Patrick Stephens Ltd, 1972-76.

Moody, Bert. *Ocean Ships.* London: Ian Allan Ltd, 1971.

Sawyer, L. A. & Mitchell, W. H. *From America to United States (Volumes 1-4),*
Kendal, Cumbria: World Ship Society, 1979-86.

Scull, Penrose. *Great Ships Around the World.* New York: Ziff-Davis Publishing Co, 1960.

New York Port Handbook. New York: Port Authority of New York & New Jersey, 1958-81.

Ships & Sailing. Milwaukee, Wisconsin: Kalmbach Publishing Co, 1950-60.

Towline. New York: Moran Towing & Transportation Co, 1950-94.

Via Port of New York. New York: Port Authority of New York & New Jersey, 1955-95.

Night shot of Hoboken piers from a dockside water tower. *Port Authority of New York & New Jersey.*

Index